EXPERIMENTS IN COOPERATION

A SERIES OF TWENTIETH CENTURY FUND/CENTURY FOUNDATION REPORTS examining the key issues post-Soviet Russia faces as it makes the change from communism to a market economy and struggles to find its place in the world.

Other papers in the series:

ECOLOGICAL DISASTER:
Cleaning up the Hidden Legacy of the Soviet Regime
by Murray Feshbach

A FAREWELL TO ARMS?
Russia's Struggle with Defense Conversion
by Kevin P. O'Prey

RUSSIA IN TRANSITION

EXPERIMENTS IN COOPERATION

ASSESSING U.S.-RUSSIAN PROGRAMS IN SCIENCE AND TECHNOLOGY

Glenn E. Schweitzer

A Twentieth Century Fund/
Century Foundation Report

1997 • The Twentieth Century Fund Press • New York

The Twentieth Century Fund sponsors and supervises timely analyses of economic policy, foreign affairs, and domestic political issues. Not-for-profit and nonpartisan, the Fund was founded in 1919 and endowed by Edward A. Filene.

Library of Congress Cataloging-in-Publication Data

Schweitzer, Glenn E., 1930–
    Experiments in cooperation: assessing U.S.-Russian programs in science and technology / Glenn E. Schweitzer.
        p. cm. -- (Russia in transition) "A Twentieth Century Fund report."
    Includes index.
    ISBN 0-87078-405-6
    1. Technical assistance, American--Russia (Federation) 2. Investments, American--Russia (Federation) 3. United States--Relations--Russia (Federation) 4. Russia (Federation)--Relations--United States. I. Title. II. Series.
HC340. 12.S39 1997
338.91' 173047--dc21   97–123
                                                                              CIP

Cover design and illustration: Claude Goodwin
Manufactured in the United States of America.

FOREWORD

After the collapse of the Soviet Union, Western officials took a moment to pinch themselves to see if they were dreaming and then turned quickly to fretting about the uncertainties created by the disappearance of familiar patterns in international politics. It is easier to parody their concerns; after all, compared to the previous life-and-death competition, all new problems were, in a sense, modest. That is not to say that some were not freighted with danger. Highest on this list of serious questions was and is the prevention of the transfer of nuclear and other weapons and components into the hands of forces that might be more hostile to the United States than our suddenly pacified longtime adversary. Moreover, the White House and Congress understood clearly that even if we could keep the weapons and materials themselves from crossing borders, scientists with the know-how to develop nuclear devices might be recruited by less advanced nations or terrorist groups.

As a sub-theme for American policy in this area, there have been a series of initiatives based on the recognition that, in some realms, Russian science has progressed to levels at least comparable to ours. Policymakers thus have thought that the United States could benefit from sharing knowledge with its former rival.

In contrast to the other papers in the Fund's Russia in Transition series, the story described in this paper is not one of frustration. Those other essays—some published, some forthcoming—detail the continuing trials of those who are attempting to assist Russia in converting its defense industries to manufacturing civilian goods, cleaning up its environment, strengthening labor unions and the laws governing them, and improving its health care system. But as Glenn Schweitzer, the director of the Office for Central Europe and Eurasia at the National Academy of Sciences, documents here, many of the joint Russian-U.S. science and technology initiatives launched since the Soviet Union's collapse have, in the main, yielded mutual benefits. Although assessments of success vary from project to project, Schweitzer persuasively shows that investments to date in cooperative science and technology ventures have been more worthwhile than in other realms.

One reason, perhaps, is the overlap between both nations' private commercial and governmental interests. Promoting the development of technology that would improve detection of earthquakes in Russia, for example, creates obvious profitable opportunities for private sector equipment manufacturers while serving the Russian public at large. From the standpoint of the United States, the project advances our nation's interests in focusing Russian scientists on peaceful domestic undertakings, modernizing a decrepit economy that might not long sustain democracy, and helping domestic manufacturers to gain a foothold in a vast and potentially lucrative market.

Further, as Schweitzer documents, cooperative initiatives in science and technology can be pursued on a relatively small scale. Costs are much lower and goals are less ambitious in comparison to the vastly more complex tasks of cleaning up chemical-infested waters or converting massive factories with obsolete machinery to commercially viable plants for manufacturing civilian goods. Indeed, the relatively low financial obligations that would accrue to the U.S. government as a result of these initiatives ought to give them a fighting chance to survive as a cost-conscious Congress hostile to foreign aid wields its budget-cutting axe.

Nonetheless, the current disdain on Capitol Hill toward foreign aid generally and toward Russia in particular does not discriminate between endeavors that have proved to be relatively successful and those that have not. Schweitzer proposes a number of sensible recommendations for continuation of government support for cooperation that would build on efforts that have worked well so far. We hope his cogent arguments are not drowned out by the anti-foreign aid chorus.

As indicated above, the Fund is pursuing a steady agenda in the evolving area of U.S.-Russian relations. In addition to the series on Russia in Transition, many of our book-length studies touch on aspects of this issue. For example, Michael Mandelbaum's important work *The Dawn of Peace in Europe* focuses on the potential effects that NATO expansion might have on that relationship. Taken together, we believe that these scholars are providing a realistic and insightful framework for other scholars, students, and policymakers. On behalf of the Trustees of the Twentieth Century Fund, I thank Glenn Schweitzer for his contribution to this effort.

RICHARD C. LEONE, *President*
The Twentieth Century Fund
February 1997

CONTENTS

ACKNOWLEDGMENTS

Your manuscript is both good and original; but the parts that are good are not original, and the parts that are original are not good.

Samuel Johnson

During the past five years, the number of scientists and engineers from Russia and the United States involved in bilateral cooperative activities has increased at least tenfold—and probably more. They are located within government agencies, research laboratories, universities, business and industry, consulting firms, foundations, and other types of organizations, both in the United States and Russia.

Whether a veteran or a newcomer to the crucibles of cooperation, each specialist makes unique contributions to relations between the two countries, with impacts beyond the confines of a single office or laboratory. These accomplished specialists are the subject of this book, and their achievements, their frustrations, and their optimism have provided the basis for the commentary on every page.

I am particularly indebted to a number of colleagues in Washington, D.C., who took the time to comment on a draft of the manuscript, and to representatives of organizations throughout the United States who reviewed the passages concerning their own specific activities. Special accolades are directed at Marilyn Pifer of the Department of State, who reviewed a very early draft, provided penetrating comments for improving the text, and helped set the diverse story lines on a sound footing.

In Russia, many colleagues graciously entertained my questions and provided both written documents and oral comments that have been very helpful in compiling this manuscript. Yuri Shiyan of the Foreign Relations Department of the Russian Academy of Sciences was particularly helpful, both in arranging very useful visits and in carrying out the survey of the views of selected Russian specialists concerning cooperative activities described in Chapter 4.

I will long be indebted to the Twentieth Century Fund, which invited me to write the book. Brewster Denny, a prime mover of the Fund's activities directed toward Russia, was particularly helpful in providing insightful comments for strengthening the book.

Also, the Rockefeller Foundation invited me to spend four weeks during the summer of 1996 at Villa Serbelloni in Bellagio, Italy. There, ideal working conditions enabled me to prepare the second draft of the manuscript as well as to complete other projects of interest to the Foundation.

And, as always, I greatly appreciated the very able assistance of my wife, Carole, who edited the manuscript during several stages of its development. Not only does she know how to ensure that the logic, structure, and details of a text are in order, but her firsthand experience in dealing with many American and Russian scientists in Moscow resulted in numerous excellent suggestions as to how the situation in a country in turmoil could be accurately portrayed.

PROLOGUE

The Freedom Support Act is a once in a century opportunity to advance our national interests.

Former Secretary of State James Baker
April 1992

Are you helping us, or are we helping you?

Official of Russian Agency for
Cooperation and Development
September 1993

FOREIGN AID, SCIENTIFIC SYMPATHY, OR GENUINE COOPERATION

The past five years have witnessed a rapid expansion of bilateral programs that have drawn on the skills and experiences of American and Russian scientists and engineers.[1] U.S. Government agencies have committed more than $2.6 billion (see Appendix A) to the support of programs that call for scientists and engineers to play critical roles in carrying out project activities.[2] In addition, the American private sector, with the strong encouragement of U.S. government officials, has committed more than $2 billion to activities in Russia that are being implemented by technical specialists from the two countries.[3]

For Russia's part, almost every government agency and sizable scientific, engineering, and educational organization has invested scarce financial resources in efforts to attract and retain partners from the United States and other Western countries, preferably partners prepared to provide additional financing for future cooperation. Often the central ministries have encouraged, supported, or controlled such cooperation. In addition, numerous programs have been established at *local initiative*—by regional and municipal governments and by individual enterprises

1

and institutes. During the author's numerous discussions in Russia, it has become clear that the authorities in Moscow have accrued only limited knowledge of such endeavors, over which they have surprisingly little influence.[4]

Notwithstanding an absence of reliable data, Russian officials seem convinced that their country's own commitment to joint activities has significantly exceeded the American commitment. Of course, it is the view of the U.S. government that the Russians' contributions should be substantial since most of the activities are sited in Russia with concomitant local benefits. The Russian contributions generally take the form of (1) labor of technical specialists, (2) use of existing facilities and equipment, and (3) provision of supporting services. Sometimes these contributions rely on people who have other career options, but frequently the projects draw on personnel (and equipment) that would otherwise be idle. With the downsizing of the Russian defense industry and a widespread slump throughout the scientific and industrial communities, such inventories of idle workers and facilities are overwhelming, with many resources available for joint projects.[5]

American organizations, for their part, have financed many activities on a long-term, sustained basis. Other American expenditures have been in response to opportunity targets that might or might not lead to long-term involvement. And an extraordinarily large number of *pilot* and *demonstration* projects have been undertaken, although there has been little assurance that even the highest level of "success" claimed for such a project would lead to replication of the approach that was being demonstrated.

Meanwhile, Russian partners in most joint projects, struggling to survive the immediate months ahead, give little thought to the long-term viability of programs that encompass the ventures. They are simply too strapped financially to worry about follow-on activities when it is current activities that enable them to support their families. While some American partners are increasingly sensitive to the long-term sustainability of projects, the Russian focus is almost always on the near future.

At the outset, many Russian officials and managers incorrectly assumed that American funding for Russia would simply replace the state subsidies that were rapidly disappearing. However, a relatively small portion of the American contribution to joint projects has gone to the Russian participants themselves, that being in the form of salaries for carrying out specific projects. Well over one-half of the almost $5 billion U.S. commitment to bilateral activities in science and technology has paid the costs incurred by the American participants—their salaries, travel expenses, equipment needs, and related expenditures—and the overhead costs of the American institutions where they are employed. Sometimes the American institutions waive or ignore personnel and overhead costs in their official calculations of expenditures, but usually these costs are included.[6]

Another large portion of the U.S. financing has been used to purchase equipment in the United States for shipment to Russia. Usually the items have been helpful, but there are many instances in which imported items were not as appropriate for projects as equipment already available in Russia, in terms of both technical capabilities and ease of maintenance. In a few extreme cases, foreign equipment that has arrived in Russia has been of little interest to the Russians. Occasionally, but not often, American funds have been used to purchase goods in Russia.[7]

The two other large categories of expenditures, each amounting to perhaps 10 percent of the total American contribution, have supported the international travel and related business expenses of Russian participants in projects and, as noted above, the salaries of some of these participants.[8] The unprecedented amount of travel—in both directions—for developing and carrying out cooperative projects has led to charges of nuclear, ecological, and scientific "tourism." One would hope that such charges are valid in only a very few cases.

The oversimplified budget profile presented here reflects a program mix consisting of *technical assistance*, with large expenditures for American consultants; *foreign investment*, with American companies emphasizing management and marketing services and purchases of equipment as their contributions to joint ventures and subsidiary operations; and *collaboration*, with American and Russian counterparts each contributing financial and in-kind resources to the extent they are able.

At the project level, there is seldom a clear division between technical assistance, investment, and collaboration. Regardless of the formal classifications, many Russian organizations are particularly sensitive to the use of the term "foreign aid" in reference to any kind of collaborative support. They are convinced that they have a great deal to bring to the table whatever the character of the project, and their conviction is usually justified. At the same time, though, few Russian institutions are in a position to serve as equal partners in providing the cash necessary for their share of operational expenses. They often rationalize such an imbalance as temporary indebtedness to be repaid in the future.

No matter how even or uneven the stacks of collaborative chips, many Americans travel to Russia with a sympathetic orientation toward the economic plight of their colleagues and a readiness to provide support beyond the strict requirements of contractual obligations. Similarly, Russian specialists sometimes become so involved in cooperative activities that they forget to limit their efforts to eight hours per day.

BENEFITING FROM JOINT ENDEAVORS

For Russian institutions, the major motivation for seeking a rapid expansion of joint American-Russian programs has been the need to find reliable sources of financing for meeting payrolls at a time of sharply declining budgets. More than one-half of civilian research programs of significance in Russia are dependent in part on foreign sources of support.[9] Indeed, in recent times it has been difficult to find a Russian laboratory that is carrying out meaningful research without the lifeline of an international connection.

In most cases, only after financing is secured do Russian scientific leaders even consider the other reasons for international cooperation. They then turn their attention to opportunities to reduce duplication of effort, to benefit technically from achievements abroad, to gain insights as to the receptiveness of world markets to the results of research and development (R&D), to address the global aspects of environmental and other problems, and to gain stature through participation in international quests for knowledge.

In the West, the reasons motivating the upsurge in cooperation in science and technology are more complex. Since 1992, American scientists have been in the forefront of Western efforts to "save Russian schools of science" in hopes that the international community will again benefit from the pioneering scientific achievements that characterized much of the research in the USSR before the onset of its economic decline. Access to Russian databases and geographical areas, including previously closed regions, continues to be a major attraction for many American institutions. Unusual opportunities to influence the direction of Russian research and education during a period of transition have also engendered widespread international interest.

Many governmental organizations in Washington, D.C., stimulated by the sudden availability of foreign assistance funds appropriated by Congress in the early 1990s in the wake of the unanticipated demise of the USSR, have activated programs or expanded their interests in Russia. Some are anxious to help Russia downsize its weapons establishment and at the same time to deflect financial incentives for Russian specialists to look to third world countries as markets for their weapons skills. American bargain hunters want to reduce the costs of their own programs by taking advantage of Russian technical achievements. In fields such as space exploration, technology that emerged from the billions of dollars of prior Soviet investments now may be available at low cost. In other areas, the low salaries of Russian specialists have led to very inexpensive projects by Western standards. Also, the U.S. and other governments are motivated to take action in Russia to help prevent nuclear accidents, nuclear theft, and the spreading of environmental pollutants or diseases beyond the country's borders.

Despite an often unfriendly business environment, American firms continue to be enticed by the lure of Russian natural resources, of an undeveloped and potentially large market for consumer products, and of a highly skilled but underutilized manpower pool. Many chief executive officers of American companies are on the alert for previously unexposed Russian brainpower, test facilities, and technological achievements that can complement the capabilities of their own companies. Some American entrepreneurs are even establishing new, university-level educational institutions in Moscow to tap into the financial resources of the emerging wealthy class of Russians demanding market-oriented curricula.

Greatly confusing the approaches from the West in general, and the United States in particular, has been the involvement in Russia for the first time of foreign assistance organizations such as the U.S. Agency for International Development (AID), the European Commission's Technical Assistance Program (TACIS), the World Bank, and the development programs of a host of other UN agencies. These organizations and their contractors have introduced into Russia unfamiliar development agendas expounded by many specialists accustomed to dealing with third world countries.

The foreign aid practitioners, determined to reshape Russia, have rallied behind a call for projects that promote systemic *reform that is sustainable*. To some American scientists, this unfamiliar slogan means encouraging the Russian government to install peer-review systems, to finance specific projects at research institutes rather than to subsidize all activities within the entire institution, and to transfer from Russian research establishments to municipal authorities their traditional responsibilities for maintaining schools, housing, and recreational facilities. These goals, modest as they were, fell far short of the development agencies' ambitions. Meanwhile, a few veteran Kremlin watchers question whether American efforts to inoculate the very fiber of Russian society with Western-style reform vaccines can ever be decisive in conditioning a healthy Russia.

Armed with experiences of questionable relevance to Russia, American assistance experts descended en masse in Moscow beginning in 1992. At that time, they were convinced, for example, that electrification schemes developed in Pakistan were just what was needed in Russia, that bankrupt privatized firms were better than subsidized state firms, and that Internet connections should be supported only to the extent that they link together organizations that advertise themselves as *forces for democracy.* And overarching such views has been the conviction of most Western development agencies that foreign advisers are the key to success in Russia.[10]

That said, these experts have gradually accepted the reality that Russia is simply different from other countries that thrive on technical assistance and that foreign advisers only make sense if someone is interested in advice. After a number of false starts and revised agendas, the assistance agencies have sponsored many projects of genuine interest to the Russian government and the Russian people, particularly in recent months.[11]

With such a mixture of players and agendas, cooperative activities take on many forms. Professional exchanges, training programs in Russia and abroad, preparation of draft laws and new textbooks, parallel and joint research programs, financial support for Russian researchers, purchases of technologies and reports prepared in Russia, and employment of Russian specialists in assembly or production of high-technology products are just a few of the many mechanisms that are being employed. Programs are undertaken for three months, for three years, or for even longer periods. Some programs involve expenditures of millions of dollars, others thousands of dollars. Some programs call for high levels of foreign intrusiveness into financial dealings of Russian organizations and for foreign access to sensitive Russian defense facilities. Others are characterized by a hands-off Western attitude concerning the internal financial and administrative activities of Russian organizations.

SUCCESS IN THE EYE OF THE BEHOLDER

Against this background of diverse interests, what can be said as to whether cooperative programs in science and technology have succeeded or failed during the past several years? That depends naturally upon how success is defined. Each program contains its own objectives, sometimes very general and sometimes quite specific. Each raises different expectations. Thus, comparing project objectives and outcomes—or, in the narrow program sense, comparing the costs of the inputs with the value of the outputs—is important. But this type of evaluation is only a first step.[12]

For some American foreign policy officials, an equally important issue is whether an education or research program has contributed, directly or indirectly, to the general objective of supporting Russia's movement toward an open and pluralistic democratic society, toward adoption of a competitive market economy, and toward becoming a responsible member of the international community. While explicit program objectives may not address such lofty, long-term goals, the compatibility of even very narrow programmatic aims with political and economic goals may be important, so these officials argue.

Of course, the science policy experts will ask whether American projects have been significant in reinforcing Russia's efforts to maintain a research and development base that can contribute both to the advancement of international science and to the country's own economic progress. And they will inquire as to whether U.S. efforts have favorably influenced Russia's attempts to *restructure* its national science and technology base.

Even in cases where such broad political interest is absent, the impacts that are felt beyond the limited scope of many programs are often very important. Thus, for an exchange program, the concern is not merely how many Russians successfully completed a course in the United States. Other important questions are: How influential were the individual participants when they returned home? Which exchange experiences, if any, had direct relevance to their professional responsibilities in a setting entirely different from that projected in the course? To what extent have they then been able to apply the insights they gained overseas?

For cooperative research projects, one might reasonably ask whether the Russian participants remained active members of international networks of scientists after completion of the programs and whether the significance of these international linkages goes further than simply sharing the details of scientific investigations. Have Russian scientists who participated in joint programs provided new ideas for improving Western experimental procedures? If so, were such procedures in the United States modified over time? For an environmental assessment program, the issue should not be restricted to how the analysis was conducted, but should be framed in terms of whether it resulted in action to attack environmental problems. Finally, a U.S. company will surely ask whether gifts of equipment to a Russian educational institution led eventually to purchases of its products by the institution's graduates and their colleagues.

In the context of Russian pragmatism—with concern for survival paramount—institute directors, as noted, judge the success of cooperating with the West in terms of positive cash flow to their institutions. While lower-level researchers are also concerned about the financial dimension, they may be more interested in gaining international recognition for their achievements at a time when no one in Russia seems to care whether or not they show up for work.

In short, different groups will measure success in different ways. For the participating scientists, success may be linked to whether the interactions increased the number and quality of their research publications. For Western governments, the inevitable test is whether the programs influenced political behavior on the other side. And for businesses, the ultimate measure of the value of their involvement in Russia will be the influence on profits.

Realistically, the judgment of success or failure will in large measure vary according to the eye of the beholder. If the governments, the funders, the project entrepreneurs, the client institutions, and the participants are satisfied with the results of a program, the program would appear to have achieved its purposes. But even in these cases, questions over scientific tourism will often linger unless it can be demonstrated that the program made an easily discernible difference in Russia or the United States.

Of course, it is unfair to compare program achievements against a hypothetical standard of absolute perfection, particularly in Russia with so many unpredictable forces influencing joint projects. However, using project accomplishments of the late 1980s as the baseline, the activities of the past several years have encompassed many breakthroughs in developing environments of trust and high productivity in fields of great interest to American organizations as well as to Russian collaborators. A number of these activities are described in the chapters that follow.

POLICY CROSSROADS FOR FUTURE PROGRAMS

How future political scenarios in the United States and Russia will alter the path of Russian-American science and technology cooperation during the remainder of this century is hard to predict. In Washington, D.C., and Moscow, many of the political architects who designed the original landscape for cooperation in 1991 and 1992 have moved on, and their successors are operating in different political environments with their own personal and professional agendas. For example:

1. Several recent political and military developments in Russia are perceived in Washington as inimical to U.S. interests. Such events have eroded bipartisan congressional support for high-intensity U.S.-Russian interactions in a wide variety of fields. Specifically, Moscow's handling of the Chechnya situation disgusted Americans, and suspicions abound as to its hidden agenda with regard to Ukraine.

2. Congress has imposed new budget constraints on many government agencies that have been involved in Russia. Also, the economic assistance program of U.S. AID, which has very large science and technology components, is being challenged in its entirety on Capitol Hill as ineffective in promoting American interests.

3. Meanwhile, many important American organizations have become heavily dependent on government funds to sustain their activities in Russia, yet these funds are rapidly disappearing. Dozens of American universities and research institutions continue to knock on doors in Washington in search of additional resources to continue their programs, while a number of U.S. companies, now accustomed to government support for their feasibility studies and to public-sector assistance in arranging financing in Russia, are suffering an unpleasant awakening to new economic realities.

4. The perennial complaints of Russian nationalists over the growing intimacy with the West have found sympathetic audiences within the Duma and even at the highest levels of the executive branch. The rhetoric of the conservative forces emphasizes the "fallacies and dangers" of international programs that "give away" Russian technologies, agreements that cede to foreigners "control" over domestic research priorities, and arrangements that ensure deeper international "penetration" of the security heartland of the country.

5. Opposition to NATO's eastward expansion has become a rallying point for Russian politicians of all stripes; their political

fervor inevitably leads to difficulties for advocates of Russian-American cooperation.

6. Economic distress and chronic budgetary shortfalls limit progress in the ratification by the Duma of arms control agreements—which come with hefty price tags for implementation—that are central to the U.S.-Russian relationship.

7. The Russian government's deals to sell nuclear reactors in Iran and elsewhere provide yet another flashpoint that jeopardizes bilateral cooperation.

8. On the positive side, a new, Washington-based, government-funded Civilian Research and Development Foundation for promoting American cooperation with Russia has come on-line. It has a broad charter but an uncertain financial future.

Apart from the diverse portfolio of intergovernmental activities, the U.S. and Russian Governments can only lament or applaud unofficial activities that fall outside their direct grasp and are somewhat immune to political changes. The International Science Foundation apparently has awarded its last grants in Russia. Its founder, George Soros, has decided to focus his interest in Russian technology on establishing Internet connections among universities in provincial cities throughout the country. The Howard Hughes Medical Institute has announced its first grants to Russian biomedical researchers, while several American professional societies continue to lend helping hands to struggling Russian colleagues.

Americans heavily populate seminars in Russia organized by the North Atlantic Treaty Organization, the Organization for Economic Cooperation and Development, the U.N. Educational, Scientific, and Cultural Organization, the World Health Organization, and other international organizations on every hot-button policy issue in science and technology. The World Bank continues to press forward with programs in the energy and environmental sectors but hesitates to embrace Russian R&D in its loan portfolio, pointing out that the Russian Ministry of Finance itself does not consider research a priority. At the same time, though, the Bank's specialists are beginning to recognize the difficulty of reforming higher education in Russia—a current prime objective—without concurrently addressing research.

Finally, American firms continue their modest probing in Russia, but many high-technology companies prefer to hold back on major investments until the entrepreneurial climate is more inviting. While Russian officials repeatedly pledge to improve the friendliness of business-related laws and policies and the security of the banking system, the combination of a proactive tax service, an expanding federal customs service, ever-growing outbreaks of crime, and burgeoning local terrorism stretch the limits of tolerance of even seasoned cynics from the Western business community.

Despite the uncertain future of U.S.-Russian relations, Vice President Al Gore and Prime Minister Viktor Chernomyrdin have continued their search for additional initiatives that can be promoted not only at their own semiannual meetings but also at summit meetings. However, with dozens of bilateral agreements involving science and technology cooperation already in place, more and more attention is being given to effective implementation rather than to new starts.

FIVE YEARS OF TRANSITION, TRAUMA, AND TOGETHERNESS

The chapters that follow describe a variety of activities that can be characterized as bilateral science and technology cooperation between American and Russian institutions and individuals. Many science and technology exchanges of importance, however, have not been captured in this effort. The array of cooperative programs is simply too extensive, involving hundreds of institutions in each of the countries, to compile a complete record of interactions. Even the visa offices of the U.S. Department of State and the Russian Ministry of Foreign Affairs are no longer authoritative sources of the traffic between the two countries since many visitors now travel on multiple-entry visas.

One very large and important area of bilateral cooperation—physical protection, control, and accountability of nuclear materials, commonly referred to as the problem of "loose nukes"—will be touched upon only very lightly in this study, as it is covered extensively in other sources.

Otherwise, the activities that are chronicled herein are representative of most of the types of cross-pollination in science and technology between the two countries from early 1992 until the end of August 1996. They provide a good point of departure for assessing, in terms of this field, where the two countries have been already and where they should be going.

Also featured in a separate chapter is a summary of the views of a number of Russian officials, scientists, and policy observers who have firsthand knowledge of cooperation. Too often Americans judge the importance of joint activities from the Washington perspective without paying enough attention to the repercussions in Russia. American-made, energy-saving streetlights, for instance, make sense in Moscow as long as they are protected from vandals; management training of Russians in the United States is important if the trainees have something to manage when they return home; and Internet connections are useful only insofar as the user charges are not excessive.

An important theme of the book is *lessons learned* during the past five years of cooperation in science and technology, including those approaches that deserve replication and those that should be avoided. While identifying new programs that work well is always refreshing, careful observation reveals that some of the most important endeavors have been under way for many years. Despite political pronouncements about removing the barriers to cooperation, long-standing administrative problems will continue to plague many projects, but preventive measures can help reduce these problems to an acceptable minimum.

The final chapter helps set the stage for future policies and programs, in anticipation of major changes as large blocks of U.S. foreign assistance funds for Russia come to an end. Much of the "peace dividend" has been spent. New mechanisms are needed to fill the void. The text suggests several such mechanisms—approaches that make clear to all concerned that Russia will no longer be a recipient of assistance but rather a genuine *partner* in cooperative ventures and that the U.S. government will support activities in Russia not because they benefit Russia but because they benefit the American taxpayer in a reasonable time frame. Thus, the Russian official's question as to "who is helping whom" should eventually be answered in full confidence that we are helping each other.

CHAPTER 1

SCIENCE, COOPERATION, AND DETENTE

Soviet society is no longer insulated from the influences and attractions of the outside world or impervious to the need for external contacts.

Henry Kissinger
March 1976

Our countries cannot afford to allow matters to reach a confrontation . . . It is necessary to stop the arms race, to tackle disarmament, to normalize Soviet-American relations.

Mikhail Gorbachev
August 1985

MARCHING TO THE BEAT OF THE DIPLOMATS' DRUMS

The first U.S.-Soviet intergovernmental agreement that called for scientific exchanges was signed in 1958 (Agreement between the United States of America and the Union of Soviet Socialist Republics on Exchanges in the Cultural, Technical, and Educational Fields). Cooperation between the academies of sciences of the two countries began one year later (Agreement on the Exchange of Scientists between the National Academy of Sciences of the USA and the Academy of Sciences of the USSR).[1]

During the next thirty years, bilateral cooperation in science and technology between the two superpowers became an important aspect of East-West relations. Political disagreements between the two governments frequently interrupted the process and the administrative uncertainty associated with the issuance of visas to participants in joint projects, including those that had been carefully negotiated by official representatives of the two governments, was a constant nuisance. Nevertheless, sustained, collaborative endeavors of American and Soviet scientists and engineers provided a small but important rudder of stability that helped offset the ebb and flow of bilateral political relations throughout the cold war, as many thousands of participants in joint science and technology efforts flew back and forth across the Atlantic Ocean (and a few hundred others traversed the Pacific) during a period of thirty years.

After a modest beginning in the late 1950s, a flurry of intergovernmental agreements in the mid-1960s led to a significant increase in annual exchanges involving several dozen specialists in each country. The areas of interest included space exploration, atomic energy, desalination technology, medical sciences, fisheries research, agricultural research, computer technology, and building construction. Painstakingly negotiated arrangements, usually including all details of travel itineraries, were often essential as both sides protected their military secrets. The Americans carefully guarded other industrial secrets lest cooperation help the economy of the Soviet Union, while Soviet officials limited travel to the United States largely to the party faithful.

Then, in the early 1970s, Secretary of State Henry Kissinger entered the picture. As noted by the author in an earlier book:

> Kissinger launched a decade of expanded bilateral scientific and technological cooperation as one of the centerpieces of U.S. efforts to improve relations between the two countries. This cooperation was brought to life in eleven formal intergovernmental agreements in science and technology. These programs had the desired political effect of translating the concept of detente into highly visible terms. In some cases they resulted in discernible advances in science and technology. At the same time, the cost of this cooperation was insignificant in comparison with the expenditures on science and technology directed to military confrontations—millions versus tens of billions of dollars.[2]

In 1975, the docking of the Apollo and Soyuz space vehicles dramatically highlighted the political payoff from cooperative ventures as envisioned by Kissinger. The majority of the populations in both countries gained new respect for the technological capabilities of political adversaries while rejoicing that perhaps detente could become a reality.

Within a few years, however, scientific cooperation was no longer politically correct. The negative U.S. reaction to the Soviet intervention in

Afghanistan in 1979 and the subsequent boycotts of the Moscow and Los Angeles Olympic Games in 1980 and 1984 set back the cause of collaboration. The downing of Korean airliner KAL 007 by the Soviet Air Force resulted in termination of several joint commissions. Also, brutal Soviet treatment of human rights advocates had a chilling effect on American enthusiasm for technical exchanges, particularly since some Soviet dissidents were prominent scientists.

Finally, with the ascendancy of Mikhail Gorbachev in the mid-1980s and concurrent bilateral progress on arms control and human rights issues, cooperation in science and technology again became a popular form of demonstrating pleasure with the positive developments in East-West relations. At the same time, though, many senior U.S. officials serving in the Republican administrations of the 1980s became uneasy with the possibility that such exchanges could result in access to sensitive American technical achievements. Consequently, the technological gains and losses from exchanges—in addition to their political acceptability—became a key consideration for approval in Washington, particularly if the U.S. government was to cover part or all of the costs of a proposed joint project.

GOVERNMENTAL MONITORING OF COOPERATION
TO ENSURE MUTUAL BENEFITS

Prior to the Gorbachev era, U.S. government agencies played lead roles in most cooperative activities in science and technology. The agencies negotiated with Soviet counterparts the areas for cooperation, worked out the details of the arrangements, and selected the American participants. While exchange programs sponsored by the National Science Foundation, including the program administered by the National Academy of Sciences, involved national competitions for selection of the American participants, the two governments set the broad outlines of the programs and retained the right of review. On occasion, proposed activities that had passed scientific muster were not approved.

During this period, many companies and academic institutions in the United States eagerly sought their own niches in the Soviet Union, independent of government agreements. They saw there a large work force of highly qualified manpower; they were impressed by Soviet technical achievements; and they were intrigued by the possibility of working in a country on America's foreign policy frontier.

Without fanfare, a few succeeded in establishing projects that they considered very beneficial.

However, these private efforts were carefully monitored by the two governments and prospered only if they were accompanied by official endorsements in Moscow and Washington. All Soviet institutions, regardless of how they characterized themselves, were in fact governmental entities. Institutes of the Soviet Academy of Sciences, for example, were governmental laboratories; even university professors were employees of the government. On the American side, most participants from the private sector were dependent on the National Science Foundation, the Department of Energy, the U.S. Information Agency, the Department of Commerce, or other agencies for financial and political support. Then, too, the two governments tightly controlled the issuance of visas, and few activities that were not supported by the governments took place.

Most American participants in cooperative ventures—whether they were from government, industry, or academia—were excited by this new cultural adventure, and they considered their insights into the capabilities of a formidable technological power adequate reward for their efforts. Soviet participants, for their part, welcomed opportunities to travel abroad and meet colleagues whose names they had encountered in the scientific literature. Also, they looked forward to witnessing firsthand, and sometimes to copying, innovations of the Americans. Indeed, in many areas, Soviet participants in exchanges followed the leads of American counterparts when developing their own research priorities and determining their budget requirements.

INCREASED INTERESTS IN COOPERATION DURING THE GORBACHEV ERA

During the Gorbachev period, cooperation in science and technology expanded in all directions. The concepts of glasnost and perestroika once again resurrected the optimism of detente, with all its political and economic implications. In some cases, intergovernmental agreements continued to provide the frameworks for cooperation. Such agreements had become routine and often were unnecessary from the foreign policy viewpoint. However, they were frequently important documents when it came to persuading budget officials in both countries to provide funding to implement the agreed-upon programs.

At the same time, Gorbachev's apparent receptivity to new approaches inspired a flurry of nongovernmental activities. American firms suddenly took a new interest in the Soviet Union, and planeloads of company executives crossed the ocean. City-to-city and university-to-university linkages became very popular, limited only by the availability of funds. Soviet and American entrepreneurs, research executives, educators, and science administrators soon became self-acclaimed diplomatic negotiators. To many, returning home after a trip abroad with a signed memorandum of understanding or other form of agreement became a symbol of success.

While cooperation was going forward at an unprecedented rate, one significant development during the late 1980s portended a dramatic change in the nature of the process in the years ahead. Increasingly, the Soviet participants in proposed projects pleaded lack of funds. If true, this development would certainly hinder participation from their side. Many American government agencies, private-sector organizations, and individuals, in their eagerness to continue or initiate collaboration despite Soviet economic problems, began paying for both ends of cooperative arrangements. By the beginning of the 1990s, a general understanding had emerged in Moscow—and was taking root in Washington as well—that "cooperation" meant that the Americans would pay the bills for international travel and per diem expenses of both American and Soviet participants. There were exceptions, particularly if high levels of the Soviet government considered an activity to be of special interest. But usually the Americans not only covered travel costs but would also try to find funds to assist in meeting expenses incurred within the Soviet Union by their counterparts.

A TECHNOLOGY BAZAAR IN THE NEW RUSSIA

Then came the unraveling of the USSR. To many American organizations engaged in cooperative endeavors in science and technology with erstwhile Soviet institutions, the fraying of the country's fabric into fifteen independent states made little difference. They had active projects, and their partner institutions would remain in place—albeit often with different names. As long as visas were issued, the political turmoil was simply an added attraction, an incentive for Americans to travel to the region, where they could witness firsthand historical changes in the making. For other American organizations, which were accustomed to all arrangements being made for them by Moscow officials, however, the splintering of the country complicated matters as lines of authority atrophied and reliable Russian interlocutors abandoned the government for more lucrative professions elsewhere.

Some Americans felt genuine empathy for the rapidly decaying situations of their Russian colleagues and feared a serious erosion of world-class scientific capabilities. Others, while also sympathetic with personal hardships, considered the opening of the country as a new opportunity to pursue their own interests, often motivated by a belief that they could benefit from the sudden availability of Russian know-how. Americans who were newcomers to the streets of Russia, whatever their motivations, thought they could "cut deals" at any level without the necessity of complicated clearances through the central bureaucracies in Moscow. But in the new environment, many dream deals quickly soured into haunting nightmares.

Russian organizations became desperate for funds from any source, and most looked to the United States as the largest and most sympathetic piggy bank. Within a short time, plant managers, research institute directors, and university rectors were no longer content to wait until the next American visitor knocked on the door. Too many of these visitors were U.S. government officials on "orientation" visits, academics in search of data, or speculators trying to find quick returns on minimal investments.

The Russians began crisscrossing the United States in search of partners with real money. Soon it seemed that every item in Russia was for sale, from formerly secret "star wars" devices to prime office space in the buildings of research institutes to the brains of the most talented Russian employees. Hard currency was the new password.

Many Americans were taken aback by the sudden appearance of a science and technology bazaar in Russia. Some were eager to sift through the many offerings until they found those technologies that would return large profits. Others wanted the U.S. government to cover their expenses for exploratory trips and feasibility studies and to guarantee that their investments would not be arbitrarily seized or diverted by Russian institutions. Still others were determined to mobilize assistance for Russia in hopes of saving the technological jewels of the former Soviet empire.

Despite crime and corruption, a lack of adequate laws governing real estate and intellectual property, and constant hassles over taxes and customs in Russia, the lure of the country was simply too tempting for thousands of Americans with interests in science and technology to resist.

Then, too, there was the added incentive of large sums of bilateral and multilateral assistance being made available to Westerners with the *right* projects. Russia—and particularly Moscow—soon became a magnet for American scientists and engineers, from all disciplines and from all types of organizations, in search of new cooperative opportunities with America's former adversary.

THE CALLS TO SAVE RUSSIAN SCIENCE

By early 1992, several months after the dissolution of the USSR, reports from Russia of meager and often unpaid salaries for scientists, cancelled subscriptions for foreign journals, inoperative experimental equipment, disconnected telephones, lack of heat in laboratories, and other deprivations had become widespread. Sympathetic American colleagues were calling with loud voices for the powers in Washington to take the lead in saving Russian science, lest well-known schools of science be lost forever. They argued that Russian scientists had made innumerable contributions of great importance to the international community; for a relative pittance the United States could ensure that future contributions would also take place. In the absence of prompt American action, its advocates predicted a massive brain drain from the country and a large exodus from science of many of the brightest young researchers.

No one disputed the financial plight of Russian scientists. Foreign aid to large numbers of world-class scientists, however, was a new concept. Surely the U.S. Agency for International Development (AID) would be reluctant to support activities with payoffs as unpredictable as those from scientific research. A skeptical U.S. Congress initially was especially hesitant about assistance to Russia that did not have near-term payoff.

Nevertheless, in early 1992 the Assistant to the President for Science and Technology requested that the National Academy of Sciences bring together leading specialists from throughout the United States and recommend a course of action for the government. The report to the White House that emerged from the meeting set forth a variety of recommendations:

1. *Weapons scientists and engineers.* The Nunn-Lugar legislation, which is described in Chapter 2, should provide research opportunities for former Soviet weapons scientists, particularly nuclear scientists, to work with the best nonweapons scientists in the

region. In this regard, the new International Science and Technology Center in Moscow should include in its programs proposals from universities and civilian research institutions as well as those from the hard-core defense establishment, recognizing that the Soviet military had penetrated many of those academic institutions. It should extend its horizons beyond nuclear weapons to other types of weapons of mass destruction and should emphasize projects that bring together former Soviet weapons and non-weapons specialists with American researchers.

2.   *Basic research.* A program for supporting civilian scientists and engineers should be established at a level of funding comparable to that for weapons scientists. The extramural research programs of several U.S. government agencies should be expanded to allow researchers to provide modest travel and spare-parts support for their colleagues in the former Soviet Union. Also, new funds should be made immediately available through the nine existing intergovernmental agreements that supported civilian R&D. Finally, a special program to help replace outmoded laboratory equipment and to renew subscriptions to foreign journals should be created.

3.   *Commercialization of technology.* The U.S. government should promptly modify its restrictive policy concerning acquisition of advanced technologies and technical expertise from the former Soviet Union by American firms, notably those with large Defense Department contracts. The fear that the U.S. firms would then be under pressure to give away their technological secrets was not well-founded. The government should also continue its efforts to reduce unnecessary export controls, particularly with regard to computers and telecommunication technologies. Foreign aid programs should facilitate conversion activities in the nonnuclear area through such mechanisms as providing venture capital for demonstration projects, subsidizing feasibility studies by U.S. firms interested in investment opportunities, and offering technical assistance to former Soviet enterprises that are assessing marketing and technical opportunities. Finally, Russian officials should be encouraged to enact legislation defining ownership rights in real estate and intellectual property, to eliminate the tax on the foreign currency

provided to support R&D, and to continue on the path to ruble convertibility and privatization.

4. *Interdisciplinary, problem-oriented research.* Washington should examine science and technology opportunities associated with the president's proposals for assistance in agriculture, health, and energy. Significantly expanded cooperation in environmental research should support sustainable development initiatives and enhance international efforts to understand changes in the global climate. In addition, U.S. agencies should be permitted to enter into research contracts with laboratories in Russia when such contracts are cost-effective.

In retrospect, this report turned out to be an unusually perceptive document.[3] While many of the ideas had been discussed previously within and outside government, the report effectively presented many recommendations that were almost immediately translated into action programs. Fortunately, among the participants at the meeting convened by the National Academy of Sciences were many U.S. specialists who would soon be in positions to carry the recommendations forward within or in close cooperation with the government. Later chapters of this book chronicle some of the projects that received significant impetus during that meeting.

A New Environment for Cooperation

Money quickly became the single most important consideration in establishing cooperative projects in Russia. Every Russian entity was in trouble financially and was searching for new sources of funding—to meet its payroll, to maintain its physical plant and respond to other overhead costs, and to supplement the meager salaries of directors and researchers.

A popular belief among American visitors to Russia was that the Russians would agree to anything for money. While this was an exaggeration, even Russian ministry officials became more willing than ever before to entertain propositions for parting with technological achievements, some of which, they figured, incorporated tens of millions of dollars of past research investments. The ministry officials, along with the directors of enterprises and institutes, had effectively lost much of their own salaries and most of their perquisites; they were determined to profit from the new wave of cooperation. Thus, it was not unusual for there to be substantial admission fees for Americans even to meet with appropriate officials or significant charges for copies of public documents that were in increasingly short supply.

The technical credentials of American individuals and organizations seeking partners became less and less important in Moscow, St. Petersburg, and other Russian cities. The power of their checkbooks was now the critical criterion. While preferring to deal with well-established American companies and research organizations, Russian entities soon had an array of agreements with lesser-known American institutions, including newly established outfits with activities limited to Russia.

OLD AND NEW MENUS FOR COOPERATION

Many modes of cooperation developed during this period of exploding interactions. Some approaches had been successfully employed for decades, while others represented new twists on Russian-American joint activities. One catalogue of collaborative ventures, efforts that varied widely depending on the Russian and foreign organizations that were involved, was prepared by the Organization for Economic Cooperation and Development:

- Personnel exchanges (high-level—one to three months; post doctoral—three to twelve months; predoctoral—twelve to twenty-four months);

- Twinning of research institutes;

- Colloquia, conferences, and summer schools;

- Science and technology components of programs in privatization and conversion;

- Technical assistance projects and expert missions to Russia;

- Mechanisms for validation and sales of Russian technologies;

- Resident Western experts to assist in project development;

- Foreign participation in development of technology parks and incubators;

- Subcontracting with Russian institutions for components of large-scale projects being implemented in the West in fields such as medicine, nuclear science, and space.[4]

In view of the many administrative uncertainties that accompanied the transition process within Russia, the motto of most American entrepreneurs trying to establish a foothold quickly became "whatever works." Surprisingly, many of the most unorthodox approaches proved to be the most effective, as will become clear in the further examination of specific projects.

CHAPTER 2

THE U.S. PROGRAM FRAMEWORK FOR COOPERATION

From joint projects far away in space . . . to innovative partnerships closer to earth . . . scientific and technological cooperation between our nations has reached a level of vibrancy and complexity that shows how much stronger we are working together.

Vice President Al Gore
Moscow, July 1996

FINANCIAL RESPONSES TO POLITICAL TURMOIL

As the Soviet Union fell apart, the U.S. Congress quickly approved two programs to provide support for the newly independent states of the former Soviet Union in making the transition to stable democracies. The *Soviet Nuclear Threat Reduction Act of 1991* (referred to as the Nunn-Lugar initiative) and the *Freedom for Russia and Emerging Eurasian Democracies and Open Markets Support Act of 1992* (referred to as the Freedom Support Act) provided the financial underpinnings for a wide variety of new programs involving Russia to be undertaken during the 1990s.[1]

In 1993, the incoming Democratic administration and the new congressional leadership decided to continue the high priority for "assistance" for Russia reflected in the two statutes adopted in the previous administration, determined to use American funds in the first instance to facilitate military, political, and economic change in the country. Dozens of additional cooperative programs were being promoted by

U.S. agencies as well, as America's political stake and its interests in the technological resources of Russia and of the other former Soviet states continued to increase.

Many of the new programs in science and technology were still in their formative stages at the outset of the Clinton presidency. They were being implemented at a relatively low level within the executive branch. Thus, they escaped serious political scrutiny—that is, there was no examination of whether they were "directly linked" to the high-priority objectives of building democratic institutions, promoting economic reform policies, facilitating privatization, and reducing the nuclear threat. Both emerging programs and long-established activities in science and technology received support as the executive branch scrambled to fill its assistance portfolios with projects that could be implemented quickly. Meanwhile, at the highest levels of government, decisions were made to encourage both the American research community and the industrial sector to expand their access to advanced technologies that had been developed within the Soviet military-industrial complex.

By 1996, Congress had appropriated more than $18 billion for "assistance" to the successor states of the Soviet Union, including direct grant assistance, credits, food grants, and food and medical donations. Most of these funds, perhaps 60 percent, were targeted to Russia.[2] Sums topping $1.5 billion have been directed to Russian science and technology activities as previously defined. If other types of relevant congressional appropriations are added to the total, more than $3 billion of public funds have been available to U.S. agencies to support projects in science and technology. Adding in the financial commitments of the U.S. private sector, the total American contribution toward redirecting Russian technical know-how in directions that meet American as well as Russian interests has approached $5 billion.[3]

The articulated assistance priorities of the U.S. government since 1992 have been (1) transition to a new security regime, (2) creation of free markets and privatization, (3) democratic institution building, and (4) emergency humanitarian and medical assistance.[4] Almost all science and technology activities funded through assistance programs have been categorized by the government as supporting the first objective (for example, certain demilitarization, nonproliferation, and defense conversion initiatives) or the second (selected trade and investment activities and health, energy, and environmental programs). The second category has been interpreted very broadly in order to include Russian priorities as well as areas of opportunity that were not anticipated when the objectives were originally developed.

Cooperative Threat Reduction Program (Nunn-Lugar)

The first pillar supporting American programs in Russia bolsters national security interests. At the urging of Senators Sam Nunn and Richard Lugar, Congress enacted legislation that called upon the Department of Defense to launch a major program directed at the successor states of the Soviet Union. This program, called the Cooperative Threat Reduction (CTR) program, has several objectives, namely:

- Facilitate the reduction of the number of nuclear, chemical, and other weapons of mass destruction within the former Soviet Union;

- Expedite transport, storage, disabling, and safeguarding of such weapons in preparation for their destruction;

- Establish verifiable safeguards against proliferation of such weapons;

- Prevent proliferation of weapons-related expertise;

- Facilitate demilitarization of defense industries and conversion of military capabilities and technologies to civilian purposes;

- Expand defense and military contacts between the United States and the successor states.[5]

In carrying out this sweeping mandate, the Department of Defense, in cooperation with other government agencies, has emphasized the following program goals:

- Upgrade the security and safety of the transport of nuclear weapons by train;

- Improve safeguards to protect weapons-grade nuclear material from theft or diversion;

- Aid in the design and construction of a secure, central facility for plutonium extracted from dismantled weapons;

- Provide assistance to eliminate Russian ballistic missiles and strategic bombers;

- Help with planning the destruction of chemical weapons and evaluate possible destruction technologies;

- Support conversion of industrial capacity for manufacturing weapons of mass destruction to civilian production;

- Reduce the incentives for transferring know-how of weapons scientists to countries of concern with respect to proliferation.

Most of these activities are dependent on the cooperative efforts of scientists and engineers from the two countries. In addition, CTR funds have been directed to studies of radioactive contamination of the Arctic, establishment of a Civilian Research and Development Foundation (discussed later in this chapter), and initiatives for promoting safety in operating nuclear reactors.[6]

ASSISTANCE UNDER THE FREEDOM SUPPORT ACT

Since Congress enacted the Freedom Support Act in late 1992, the U.S. Agency for International Development has had the primary responsibility for implementing programs of economic and technical assistance. Some programs are carried out by other government agencies, but AID plays an important role in most activities, including distributing funds to other agencies for their management and implementing of projects when appropriate.

The AID programs range across many sectors, although the agency repeatedly makes clear that its priorities are sustainable democratic systems (programs in support of free political processes, independent media, the rule of law, and local governance) and economic restructuring (programs in support of fiscal management reform, sound monetary policies, modern banking methods, and the transition to a market environment).[7] Science and technology has never been explicitly recognized as an important program area, but technology-oriented activities are subsumed under other classifications as indicated by the following examples.

1. *Energy Efficiency.* Technical assistance efforts have targeted gas distribution systems in municipal areas and safety in coal mines. Studies have been directed to formulating national alternative energy strategies. Training programs have emphasized the safety aspects of nuclear reactors, including risk reduction measures and fire safety system upgrades. Other areas of interest have included

establishing an oil and gas technology transfer center in Siberia, processing geological information for use by Western oil companies, extending the life of thermal and hydropower plants, and reducing sulfur and nitrogen emissions from coal combustion.[8]

2. *Environmental Policy.* The principal effort in the environmental field has been a series of demonstration projects, namely, Industrial Environmental Management (Nizhniy Tagil), Water Quality and Small Watershed Management (Moscow), Air Quality Management (Volgograd), Sustainable Natural Resource Management (Far East), and Multiple Pollution Sources Management (Novokuznetsk). In addition, a program of sustainable land-use planning for the Lake Baikal area is under way. Support is provided for environmental economics and risk assessment studies, and small grants are awarded to nongovernmental environmental organizations.[9] Also, equipment is being provided to strengthen the capabilities of environmental agencies in monitoring and measurement.[10]

3. *Health.* The health sector has attracted the attention of AID from the start. Of particular interest is the possibility of an acceleration of U.S. investment in the production and distribution of drugs in Russia, encouraged by means of guaranteed purchases by Russian government agencies of such drugs. AID has supported partnerships between American and Russian hospitals, and advice is being provided on improving the efficiency, accessibility, and sustainability of health services delivery. In the area of environmental health, the aforementioned environmental demonstration projects are being supplemented with efforts to strengthen Russian capabilities in the areas of risk assessment and environmental epidemiology.[11]

4. *Exchanges and Training.* The United States Information Agency (USIA) carries out graduate and undergraduate exchanges, sister university programs, and other private-sector exchanges, with thousands of Russians participating in programs oriented toward science and technology. The International Research and Exchanges Board administers twenty-two institutional partnership arrangements involving many American universities, which pursue activities in science and technology as well as in other fields. The Academy for Educational

Development organizes highly specialized training programs in the United States in technical areas of special relevance for Russia. The National Academy of Sciences provides grants to individual Russian scientists and engineers to conduct collaborative applied research for six to twelve months in the United States.[12]

UTILIZATION OF THE AEROSPACE CAPABILITY OF RUSSIA

Heading the list of other U.S. agency-initiated programs designed to draw on Russian know-how is NASA's commitment of $400 million in support of the Shuttle-Mir program. This ambitious program involves a series of complicated docking missions that will serve as a valuable precursor to the international space station. A small but important component of the Shuttle-Mir effort is a research grants program that enables Russian scientists to initiate peer-reviewed and -approved investigations relating to the space station. In fending off critics who prefer that NASA spend such large sums of money in the United States, the agency persuasively points out the large cost savings in using the excellent Russian capabilities in many areas of direct relevance to the objectives of the U.S. human space flight program.

A second major cooperative activity of NASA and Russian counterpart organizations is research on global change. The use of space-based sensors together with surface measurements provides measurements of the behavior of the earth's atmosphere, ice and oceans, land surface, interior, and biota, as well as indicators of human-induced changes on our environment. The various elements of this extensive joint undertaking are summarized in Appendix B.

A partial list of further areas of NASA-supported cooperation in the aeronautical and space sciences includes:

- Equipping a Russian TU-144LL Flying Research Laboratory for investigating technical aspects of civil supersonic transport.

- Testing a Russian scramjet engine to improve air-breathing, hypersonic engine technology.

- Aeronautical investigations of advanced metals, composite structures, application of flamelet models of supersonic combustions, atmospheric effects of aviation, boundary layer transitions, and supersonic leading edge receptivity.

- Coordination of U.S. and Russian Mars missions.

- Establishment of a space biomedical center for training and research at Moscow State University.

- Russian participation in the international program led by the United States to put an alpha magnetic spectrometer in space.

- NASA provision of several instruments and the data archiving system for the Russian Spectrum X-gamma astrophysics observatory mission.

- NASA participation in and supply of ground tracking requirements for the operation of the Russian RADIOASTRON astrophysics observatory mission.

These and other activities are carried out pursuant to various bilateral agreements dating back to the 1960s. A long history of mutual respect and trust at the institutional and interpersonal levels has helped ensure that technical projects move forward with a minimum of diversions and a maximum of political support. A NASA government/contractor team of about three dozen resident specialists in Moscow assists in coordinating Shuttle-Mir and space station activities.[13]

OTHER SCIENCE AND TECHNOLOGY PROGRAMS

More than twenty U.S. agencies have supported other cooperative programs with Russia during the past several years that have drawn heavily on the science and technology communities of the two countries. (Appendix A furnishes a listing of these.) The largest investment has been made by the Department of Defense in its "non-Nunn-Lugar" programs. Two types of activities stand out. First, many Pentagon subunits have simply purchased Russian know-how that is of interest. Two of the most widely publicized were the acquisition of the Soviet SV 300 missile and the commissioning of two hundred Russian weapons scientists to prepare a technical history of the development of Russian nuclear weaponry.[14] Also, hundreds of agreements have been inked for cooperation between American and Russian scientific institutions (many of the participating units of the Department of Defense are identified in Appendix C). The Defense Special Weapons Agency alone has entered into more than 120 contracts with Russian scientific institutions.[15]

The Department of Energy has invested heavily in bilateral science and technology projects, particularly those that are important for arms control (for example, protection of nuclear material) and nuclear reactor safety.

It is fairly common for the agencies to use both funds they receive directly in their appropriations and other money obtained in pass-through arrangements from AID and the Department of Defense in pursuing specific objectives. The following two multiagency endeavors highlight clear government priorities and emphasize the need for close coordination of government-wide activities.

Containment and Conversion of the Nuclear and Missile Threats

Containing Russian weapons expertise that could help rogue states acquire capabilities related to nuclear weapons or missile technologies is a problem that has received considerable attention from the U.S. government. A principal mechanism for this purpose is the International Science and Technology Center (ISTC). While the ISTC is an international organization, its projects for reorienting the research of weapons scientists to peacetime subjects are funded by individual member governments. The ISTC's portfolio now includes many activities that involve American and Russian counterpart organizations.[16] Bilateral programs of the Department of Energy (such as the Initiative for Proliferation Prevention), various branches of the Department of Defense, and NASA engage many additional Russian weapons scientists in the effort to diversify the fields of inquiry combed by Russian laboratories. About twenty thousand former Soviet weapons specialists were involved in all of these undertakings at the beginning of 1996.[17]

In a related area, the Department of Defense and the Department of Energy have sponsored several large programs that enhance Russian efforts to safeguard nuclear material, particularly separated plutonium and unirradiated, highly enriched uranium—materials that can be used directly in nuclear weapons without the need for difficult chemical processing. The on-the-ground programs in Russia complement broad diplomatic efforts by the United States to encourage the Russian government to strengthen, up to the level of acceptable international standards, safeguards and export controls over dangerous materials and technologies.[18]

Also, high on the U.S. agenda has been conversion of Russian enterprises and institutes making up part of the industrial complex that supported the development and production of nuclear weapon systems, including their delivery vehicles. AID has supported limited training and advisory services toward this end. The Arms Control and Disarmament Agency has sponsored a series of conversion seminars, and contractors of the departments of Energy and Defense are constantly searching for conversion opportunities at the facilities of Russia's Ministry of Atomic Energy.[19]

ENVIRONMENTAL PROTECTION

For nearly twenty-five years, the Environmental Protection Agency has sponsored cooperative projects with counterparts in the Soviet Union and now Russia. Over the years, these have expanded to include participation by other U.S. agencies and a number of nongovernmental organizations as well. On the Russian side, a large array of governmental entities became involved.

The United States strategy in this field addresses:

- Improvement of Russia's institutional capabilities in environmental policy and environmental management;

- Enhancement of ecosystem protection and conservation of biological diversity;

- Identification and reduction of health risks from pollution and other environmental problems;

- Support of Russia's ability to fulfill obligations of major international legal regimes;

- Promotion of American environmental technologies;

- Support of Russian capabilities in environmental research, monitoring, and data management.[20]

Training, assessment, and capacity-building activities, rather than actual cleanup efforts, have thus dominated the picture. While such undertakings are important, skeptics point out the difficulty of identifying any improvement in conditions in Russia as a result of the sizable expenditures by the United States.

Many bilateral programs that are not explicitly identified as environmental programs include substantial environmental components, for example, the American Business Center in Nizhnivartovsk, which emphasizes sales of American products and services related to environmental controls in the oil industry; the Initiative for Proliferation Prevention, noted previously, which has funded many environmental projects; and the programs of the Department of Defense concerning assessment of the contamination of military bases.

TRADE AND INVESTMENT

Another major thrust of Washington's program approach has provided financial incentives and support to the private sector to help increase trade and investment opportunities in Russia, often relying on American engineering skills. Some funds have been channeled through AID and some through the CTR program, but the bulk of the funding is now included in the budgets of particular agencies.

DEPARTMENT OF COMMERCE

The Department of Commerce supports a number of special activities intended to help open up new opportunities for American companies in Russia, in addition to the department's traditional services for facilitating commercial interests. These provide training to Russian managers, information services to American firms concerning the legal and business environment, advice to Russian authorities concerning compliance with international export control norms, and special trade missions devoted to the health sector. (These activities are described in Appendix D.) Of course, only a portion of such activities could be classified as science and technology programs. However, during 1995 and 1996 an increasing number of technology-oriented American companies have become seriously interested in business opportunities in Russia.

OVERSEAS PRIVATE INVESTMENT CORPORATION (OPIC)

OPIC provides three types of services. It operates like an investment bank, customizing and structuring complete financial packages for projects. It provides political risk insurance against loss due to expropriation and political violence. It sponsors missions to help American businesses explore investment opportunities. OPIC has supported many technology-based projects in Russia involving American investments exceeding $1 billion. (Examples of such projects are set forth in Appendix D.)

EXPORT IMPORT BANK (EXIMBANK)

ExImBank insures U.S. exporters and their banks against risks of nonpayment by foreign buyers. The program is designed for the sale of consumable goods, raw materials, commodities, spare parts, components, and services. A sampling of transactions covered would include services provided by Stone and Webster Engineering Corporation in the petroleum industry, computer equipment furnished by Cray Research, biochemical equipment supplied by Beckman Instruments, and turbine compressors delivered by Cooper Rolls. In addition, ExImBank is working with Russia's Ministry of Fuel and Energy to provide up to $2 billion in financing of U.S. capital exports to help restore oil and gas production and hence increase exports from Russian fields.[21]

ENTERPRISE FUNDS

The Fund for Large Enterprises in Russia was designed by the U.S. government to meet needs of medium-to-large enterprises in certain reform-oriented regions of Russia requiring access to equity and loan capital as they emerge from the privatization process. An earlier sibling, Russian-American Enterprise Fund, targeted small to medium-sized enterprises. The two have now merged to form the U.S.-Russia Investment Fund. Another institution, the Defense Enterprise Fund, supports conversion activities, particularly in Russia. Generally, the managers of these funds find investments in science and advanced technology too risky. Nevertheless they have been interested in projects concerning aircraft environmental control systems, computer software development, and irradiation techniques for preserving logs.[22]

TRADE AND DEVELOPMENT AGENCY (TDA)

TDA has given a number of grants, on a cost-sharing basis, for U.S. firms to carry out feasibility studies and other planning services needed to gain financing for major technology-oriented projects from organizations such as OPIC, ExImBank, the World Bank, and the European Bank for Reconstruction and Development. Not only Russian organizations should benefit, for such studies help open doors to continued involvement by U.S. firms. TDA's priorities in Russia include oil and gas, power plants and distribution networks, health care, transportation infrastructure, defense conversion, and electronics. (Illustrative feasibility studies are set forth in Appendix D.)

OTHER INTERESTS OF THE AMERICAN PRIVATE SECTOR

While the private sector plays a key role in many publicly funded programs, its interests antedate by decades the recently initiated government programs. The breadth of private-sector interest in opportunities in Russia related to science and technology has always been extensive.

BUSINESS OPPORTUNITIES FOR AMERICAN COMPANIES

American engineering companies have been conducting business in the Soviet Union and its successors since the 1920s. The construction of automobile plants, hydroelectric dams, and fertilizer plants drew on American industrial skills with hundreds of American engineers working in the region, prior to World War II. Then, during the dreariest political days of the cold war, some American businessmen persisted in their efforts in Russia. And for many years the former Soviet-American Economic and Trade Council, with offices in New York and Moscow, provided a forum for regular consultations on investment and sales opportunities between Russian officials and American businessmen. In 1996, more than 1,500 American companies were registered to operate in Russia. The few technology-oriented companies that have made investments exceeding $10 million in Russia have been interested primarily in the extractive industries, such as oil, gas, and aluminum, and in the aerospace sector. Some companies now considering significant investments are relying increasingly on government programs for partial support.[23]

But a few companies prefer to proceed on their own with minimum involvement of U.S. agencies. Of course, they welcome the efforts of those agencies to persuade Moscow to establish a more business-friendly environment. And they do not hesitate to bring to the attention of the two governments the many problems they encounter in Russia.

In trying to capitalize on the technological capabilities of Russia, the approaches of American companies are manifold. They buy products or licenses. They set up joint ventures in Russia or even in the United States. They hire Russian technical personnel or sign contracts with Russian organizations. They provide research grants to Russian institutions. And they organize many familiarization visits in both directions coupled with seminars and workshops. Many trade associations, both in the United States and Russia, stay abreast of developments in the two countries so their members will have fewer difficulties than would otherwise be the case.

NEW INTERESTS OF THE AEROSPACE COMPANIES

With an eye to NASA's interests in space and aeronautics technologies, the U.S. government has strongly encouraged American aerospace firms to take advantage of the well-equipped laboratories and test facilities in Russia, through research and testing contracts. Also, American firms have established joint ventures to capitalize on Russian experience in the design and construction of aircraft for the civil market and of boosters that can be used in space programs.

For instance, in space technology, several major joint projects are under way at the Khrunichev State Research and Production Space Center. In 1993, the Lockheed-Khrunichev-Energia joint venture was established to manage and market the Proton rocket booster for launching foreign satellites. Drawing on Russian expertise at Khrunichev, Motorola intends to launch twenty-one satellites under the Iridium project, and Loral is considering launching another array of satellites. Lockheed Martin and Hughes have expressed interest in the capabilities at Khrunichev as well. Meanwhile, Khrunichev is producing the first element of the international space station, the functional cargo block, under a contract with the Boeing Company.[24]

Other examples of American interest in Russian space technologies include a partnership between the Pratt and Whitney Company and Energomash that dates back to 1992 and a joint enterprise of the Aerojet Company and Dvigateli NK. Both ventures are interested in opportunities for modernizing American rocket engines.[25]

In the aircraft industry, Pratt and Whitney has entered into several arrangements to develop aircraft engines in Russia, and General Electric has aligned itself with helicopter manufacturers. Gulfstream is also producing small jets for the Russian market in cooperation with Russian partners.[26]

TECHNOLOGY BROKERS

In the early 1980s, the American press was rich with stories about Soviet techno-bandits operating in Silicon Valley. In an effort to prevent transfer of advanced technologies to the USSR, the Department of

Defense increasingly denied visas to Soviet attendees for scientific conferences in the United States. But one organization in Washington, D.C., Kiser Research, was attempting to broker reverse technology transfer—from the Soviet Union to the United States. Now, such brokering is big business, at least in the Washington area. Aside from the activities of American and Russian trade associations, several organizational patterns have become apparent as companies attempt to exploit international technology differentials.

American Commercial Brokers. A few Russian emigrés in the United States, each cultivating strong personal contacts within Russian industrial circles, offer their individual services as intermediaries in bringing together American and Russian enterprises with common business interests. They have been most successful in dealing with small American companies. As to catering to the interests of large American firms, several well-established technology brokers such as East-West Technology Partners and Kiser Research have had considerable success in bringing together American entrepreneurs with Russian institutions that have technologies for sale. Such organizations arrange visits in Russia to accustom American companies to the business climate, set up seminars in Russia, prepare analyses of Russian achievements, and respond to Russian or American requests to search out partners interested in specific technologies.[27]

Russian Sales Organizations. Russian organizations frequently act on their own to designate agents for selling technologies abroad. One of the most powerful agents is Rosvooruzheniye, the principal government-authorized organization for selling military equipment; but fighter aircraft, antiaircraft rockets, and other weapons are more likely headed to China and India than to the United States. In more modest efforts, the Russian Academy of Sciences and individual institutes have organized special entities that serve as technology channels to the world, with high hopes of penetrating the U.S. market.

Russian Brokers in the United States. On two recent occasions scientific attachés from the Russian Embassy have, at the completion of their tours of duty, established firms in the Washington area to promote scientific and technical contacts, with the specific goal of making commercial sales of Russian technology. In each case, the former diplomat has been backed by a well-placed scientist in Russia, although the extent to which such brokers in the United States can act as more than information exchange centers is not clear. In short, the success of these undertakings has yet to be demonstrated. In another approach, the well-known Central Aerohydrodynamics

Institute (TsAGI) just outside Moscow has established an outreach office in the Washington area to assist in the search for funds to support its activities.[28]

AMERICAN NONPROFIT ORGANIZATIONS

PHILANTHROPIC ORGANIZATIONS

In 1992 financier George Soros first announced his intention to establish an International Science Foundation (ISF) to provide support to scientists in the former Soviet Union. The program was to be limited to basic science and explicitly excluded scientists who had been involved in military-related activities. Through the ISF, he has provided financing of almost $130 million, with considerably more than one-half going to Russia. In the spring of 1993, the first individual "emergency" grants of $500 each were distributed to about twenty-five thousand scientists throughout the former Soviet Union.

The next round of activities of the ISF featured (a) about six thousand travel grants for Russian scientists interested in attending conferences, primarily in the United States but also in other Western countries, from 1993 to 1995; (b) 3,500 research grants on the order of $10–15,000 each for small teams of specialists throughout the region; (c) special grants to help preserve botanical collections in St. Petersburg; and (d) a demonstration of approaches to improve electronic communications among Russian scientists and between Russian and Western scientists. These programs were due to terminate at the end of 1996.[29]

A related program, the International Soros Science Education Program, provided grants to large numbers of professors, retired professors, science teachers, retired science teachers, and outstanding science students. These grants were quite small, with the usual stipend being $12,000 for two years for a distinguished professor and his or her research group.[30] Most recently, the Soros group has announced its intention to provide $100 million for Internet connections at thirty-two universities outside the Moscow and St. Petersburg areas.[31]

While the Soros programs have been by far the largest private contributions to science in Russia, several other foundations have also taken an interest in Russian scientists and the research potential embodied in their laboratories. The Sloan Foundation and the Meyer Foundation provided small levels of support to American professional societies to assist colleagues in the former Soviet Union. Then, in 1995, the Howard Hughes Medical Institute initiated a program of five-year grants of up to $30,000 per year to biomedical scientists in the region, with thirty-two grants directed to groups of Russian specialists.[32]

Several of the large American foundations—Ford Foundation, MacArthur Foundation, Carnegie Corporation—continue their support of American organizations interested in analyzing national security problems in Russia, particularly problems in the nuclear arena. These analyses usually involve the participation of Russian colleagues. Also, the MacArthur Foundation has initiated a program of small grants to Russian nongovernmental organizations, primarily in the environmental field; while the Ford Foundation concentrates on supporting social sciences.

AMERICAN UNIVERSITIES AND PROFESSIONAL SOCIETIES

Many universities and professional societies have mounted efforts to assist Russian colleagues in weathering the financial crisis that has persisted since 1991. Usually these organizations initiate small efforts with their own resources, but as soon as they realize the magnitude of the undertaking, they quickly turn to the official and nongovernmental funding sources just described.

Now many university science departments are deeply involved in Russia, with their efforts in large part underwritten by AID and the U.S. Information Agency. The universities seek further grants from the National Science Foundation (NSF) and the National Academy of Sciences to support individual Russian researchers on their campuses and to provide funding for overseas trips by faculty members.

The American Physical Society was one of the first professional associations to recognize the need to assist Russian scientific colleagues; it used internal funds to start programs. However, it soon turned to the NSF, the ISF, and other private foundations for resources to sustain its efforts. American mathematicians, astronomers, and many other specialists provided active support for their Russian colleagues. The American Association for the Advancement of Science initiated a popular program to collect and send professional journals to selected Russian institutions, but soon the cost of the program outstripped the money available, and it has since proceeded at a reduced level with some external support.[33]

A NEW FOUNDATION TO SUPPORT COOPERATION IN SCIENCE AND TECHNOLOGY

In mid-1995, NSF established the Civilian Research and Development Foundation (CRDF) in response to legislation sponsored initially by Congressman George Brown, then-Senator Al Gore, and Senator Joseph Lieberman. This nongovernmental, nonprofit organization has been assigned the following objectives:

- To provide scientists and engineers in the former Soviet Union with professional alternatives to emigration and to help prevent the dissolution of the scientific and technological infrastructure in those countries.

- To advance defense conversion by supporting collaborative civilian research projects between ex-Soviet scientists and engineers and American university and industrial researchers.

- To assist in the establishment of a market economy in the former Soviet countries sponsoring joint research and development ventures and promoting business and trade relationships.

The initial funding was $10 million, including $5 million from CTR funds and $5 million from George Soros.[34]

The leaders of the foundation hope that the new organization will become a permanent mechanism for fostering productive interactions between researchers from the United States and colleagues in the former Soviet Union at a scale significantly larger than would otherwise be possible. They believe that collaboration should improve the long-term, professional prospects of Russian participants, which will require the foundation's attention to applied, industry-oriented work as well as to basic research. While recognizing that many of the former Soviet scientific facilities are in decline, they are convinced that a substantial core of skilled scientists, particularly in Russia, will continue to have the capability to carry out research of international interest.[35]

The CRDF has received much publicity in Washington and Moscow, suggesting that it is considered by many to be a cornerstone of American-Russian collaboration in science and technology. But the level of funding available is so small that, at least in the immediate future, its impact will be limited.

The programs of the CRDF are patterned after the ISF approach, namely, solicitation of applications from scientists and scientific teams in Russia and the other successor states for one- or two-year projects in the range of $40,000 per year across a broad range of disciplines. A difference from the Soros plan is that each application must provide for an American collaborator. Awards are to be made on the basis of technical merit, with special consideration given to proposals that involve former weapons scientists and offer the possibility of near-term contributions to economic development. A small program, being implemented subsequently on a pilot basis, will provide sophisticated instrumentation, to be shared with industry, for experimenters from research establishments.[36]

INTERESTS OF THE GORE-CHERNOMYRDIN COMMISSION

The U.S. government effort to engage Russia in joint activities that will facilitate the country's transition to democracy, economic soundness, and nuclear security has been characterized by a variety of approaches. Science and technology are called upon to add strength to each of these approaches. In particular, the Freedom Support Act has provided the mandate for economic assistance. National security assistance is the domain of the Nunn-Lugar initiative. Support of private-sector trade and investment was also initially called for in the Freedom Support Act, but most of the funding has subsequently been channeled by Congress through the agencies such as OPIC and ExImBank that are most directly concerned. The extensive cooperative programs of NASA have been financed through the agency's normal appropriations procedure. These program thrusts account for more than 80 percent of the U.S. agency expenditures for joint science and technology initiatives with Russia during the past several years, with other programs of the Department of Defense and the Department of Energy accounting for most of the remainder.

Cutting across all of these activities, the Gore-Chernomyrdin Commission provides a political focal point that can energize many bilateral programs. At the Vancouver summit in April 1993, Presidents Clinton and Boris Yeltsin created a joint commission to promote a partnership based on "a shared commitment to democracy and human rights; a market economy and the rule of law; and international peace and stability."[37] In view of foreign aid appropriations, the United States had very substantial financial resources available for cooperation at the time, and the

Russian leadership was prepared to adopt almost any organizational formula that would expedite the delivery of these resources.

The commission became known as the U.S.-Russian Joint Commission on Economic and Technological Cooperation, chaired by Vice President Al Gore and Prime Minister Viktor Chernomyrdin. As suggested by the commission's very name, the links between most of the projects it embraced and "democracy and human rights" were often difficult to discern. Rather, the commission became a real boon for science and technology projects, which seemed to dominate many of the bilateral discussions. Of course, a number of projects of interest to the commission are not in the hands of scientists and engineers. Conversely, the commission never intended to embrace all bilateral activities; a significant number of science and technology cooperative projects are carried out independently, particularly those involving the Department of Defense, which often prefers to solve its bilateral problems on its own.

Originally, the commission was to "enhance cooperation in space, energy, and high technology activities."[38] During the seven sessions it held between September 1993 and July 1996, the scope of its activities expanded into a variety of areas, and eight committees were established: space, business development, energy, defense conversion, science and technology, environment, health, and agribusiness. (The heads of these committees are identified in Appendix E. To give an indication of recent interests of the commission, the thirty agreements and joint statements acted on at the commission's meeting in July 1996 are set forth in Appendix F.) Overall, dozens of projects have been brought under the umbrella of the Gore-Chernomyrdin Commission. Most involve science and technology. With each meeting, new projects are added to the portfolio. Some projects began on their own more than a decade ago and subsequently were embraced by the commission, and many of the more recent projects were also developed without commission involvement.

Russian officials have welcomed the concept of considering, at the highest levels, projects and project proposals being promoted by the various agencies of the two governments. Centralized orchestration of important activities had long been a familiar style in Moscow, and Russian advocates of cooperation thought that the prime minister, using the commission as leverage, could apply pressure on the Ministry of Finance to provide needed funding to carry out their favorite projects.

Senior American officials have been equally enthusiastic about the prospects for the commission, which in their view is designed to facilitate or fertilize businesslike bilateral interactions. They believe that the commission works because the stakes are high enough—and, simultaneously, the level of technical engagement worked out through each of the committees is deep enough—that agreements will be followed up with action, thereby signaling real progress in the development of bilateral relations.[39]

After some initial hesitancy over the establishment of yet another coordinating mechanism, most of the affected lower-level officials throughout the U.S. government have become strong supporters of the commission. There has been example after example of the commission's activism in clearing obstacles blocking the paths of agreed projects, forcing resolution of issues holding up agreements on new projects, and adding impetus to budget requests for project support in both capitals. The many glowing testimonials of long-time veterans in the Washington trenches of international science and technology cooperation policy clearly indicate that the commission has been an exceptionally successful innovation.[40]

Unfortunately, many American scientists and engineers who have no association with government but nevertheless are keenly interested in developments in Russia know little about the commission. Some consider it to be simply political symbolism, unaware that it is a body designed to push programs, including programs that could be of interest to them.

Reviewing the Coherence of the Various Cooperative Schemes

Pervasiveness of Science and Technology Programs

At one time the Soviet Union boasted that it was home to one-half of the world's engineers and one-quarter of the world's scientists. Most of these still live in Russia. Irrespective of uncertainties about the precise definitions of "scientist" and "engineer," it is obvious that technically trained professionals permeate almost every sector of Russian life. Thus, not surprisingly, many cooperative programs, intentionally or unintentionally, tilt toward science and technology.

A common reply to American scientists inquiring about funding possibilities from the U.S. Information Agency and American private foundations is, "We only support activities in the social sciences." However, many of their activities in fact extend deep into the natural sciences, particularly in relation to science education, ecological advocacy, and deployment of modern communications systems.

COORDINATION BY THE U.S. GOVERNMENT OF POLICIES AND PROGRAMS

Many offices within the executive branch attempt to keep abreast of cooperative programs. Indeed, as called for by the U.S. Congress under the Freedom Support Act, the president has appointed a special adviser on assistance to the Newly Independent States (NIS) of the former Soviet Union and coordinator of assistance to the NIS. His mandate extends far beyond assistance to include all cooperative programs (as indicated in Appendix G). The Office of the Vice President tracks activities under the Gore-Chernomyrdin Commission; the Office of Science and Technology Policy follows activities in its area of interest, which extends beyond any single committee of the Gore-Chernomyrdin Commission; the National Security Council monitors activities in its domain; and the Office of Management and Budget is interested in anything involving money—in other words, everything. At the same time, the Department of State has a responsibility to prepare an annual report on cooperative programs in science and technology and keeps its own log of such programs. (Its list of bilateral science and technology agreements is included in Appendix H.)

Despite this emphasis on coordination, several problems require prompt attention within the government. First, there is considerable confusion as to what is "assistance" and what is "cooperation." The sweeping mandate of the president's coordinator for "assistance" has caused anxieties among some program managers who do not want to be tarnished with that brush. The lack of separation between assistance and cooperation is not helpful for some U.S. agencies arguing for budget support on Capitol Hill, where "assistance" is often portrayed as an approach whose time has passed.

The perception of the meaning of "coordination" is usually in the eye of the beholder, as many individuals strive to influence not only policy directions but also project details. All agree that coordination includes keeping records on programs that are under way. While the annual and quarterly reports of the president's coordinator are helpful in this regard, they are far from complete in providing overviews of developments in science and technology cooperation. Oversight is also a function usually associated with coordination. But what is oversight, and how much more is needed? One cooperative program of the Department of Energy was subjected to oversight by nine executive and legislative bodies during a period of three months in 1996. In this context, oversight by yet another coordinator seems hard to justify.

At the same time, the president's coordinator could add value to the overall effort by concentrating on selected activities of individual agencies that fail to take into account the overall policy thrusts of the administration or the related activities of other government organizations. The Initiative for Proliferation Prevention of the Department of Energy is repeatedly criticized for duplicating at much higher costs the functions of other agencies while engaging influential Russian managers who are in demand by the other agencies as well. The coordinator is finally beginning to play a role in enhancing the benefits that should be derived from this well-funded initiative. The coordinator also played a very positive role in integrating the activities of the several enterprise funds. On the other hand, he has had little success in working the extensive non-Nunn-Lugar programs of the Department of Defense into the national agenda to cooperate with Russian scientific institutions.

REFINING THE OVERALL APPROACH

In summary, the U.S. government and private sector support a vast array of programs involving Russian and American scientists and engineers. Despite the vagueness of "science and technology" as a program classification and the subtleties of the ties to political and economic reform, many such programs are alive and well. They are receiving attention at the highest official levels. And, at the working levels, American scientific and industrial organizations regularly take the initiative to bring together American and Russian specialists from a variety of organizations working on common problems. There are a number of soft spots in fusing together the overall governmental approach, but many of these are easily correctable.

CHAPTER 3

MATCHMAKERS AT WORK

Russia was, is, and will be a great space power.
Sign at Baikanur Cosmodrome

If I can't pick mushrooms with the General Director's wife, I don't want to do business with him.
Senior American corporate officer
April 1995

RESPONDING TO THE CHALLENGES AND OPPORTUNITIES OF RUSSIA

While Russia was emerging as an independent nation during the period from 1992 to 1996, Russian and American scientists and engineers developed hundreds of joint projects. The most ambitious efforts have attracted budgets of tens of millions of dollars and engaged thousands of participants. The most modest undertakings have involved as few as two individuals and occasional airplane tickets. A large proportion of the "joint projects" were simply one-time events: a single visit, a single seminar, or a single experiment. Others have lives that will probably last for decades.

In Russia, the importance of examining the specifics in designing and implementing projects cannot be overstated. Russian and American proponents of cooperation have become expert in developing titles and descriptions for proposals that often promise more than they can deliver. Too many American enthusiasts begin ventures with a flurry of press releases and then abandon them for assignments in other countries where the frustrations are less intense. And many practitioners of cooperation on both sides of the ocean simply do not want to accept the notion that they are obligated to follow the agreed terms of their contracts. Therefore, to be meaningful, reviews of cooperative activities must give attention to the details of individual projects.

This chapter briefly discusses thirty-three joint activities that have been undertaken in recent years. Some are components of larger programs, while others stand alone. To touch on so many projects may, of course, invite criticism that such a shotgun approach provides shallow insights into the subtleties of cooperation. However, more in-depth assessments of perhaps a half-dozen projects would not begin to represent the diversity of efforts that are under way.

The thirty-three projects illustrate many types of opportunities and difficulties encountered by American organizations attempting to work in a foreign country that is experiencing dramatic political and economic convulsions. They also reflect many innovative mechanisms employed in cooperative endeavors.

In general, the joint enterprises sampled here reflect successful outcomes, at least as evaluated by the Russian and American organizations providing the necessary financial support. Thus, the representation is skewed toward undertakings trying approaches that have solved administrative and logistics problems rather than toward those that have become mired down in such problems. Indeed, the many positive aspects cited may suggest that cooperation is much easier than is really the case.[1]

Failed projects also can reveal important lessons for the future, but few participants in unsuccessful projects are willing to talk candidly about them. Thus, obtaining authoritative information on failures is not easy. Nevertheless, an assessment of trial balloons that would not fly could provide the basis for a separate book.

Undoubtedly, many endeavors not mentioned in this chapter have also been highly successful, as well as potentially instructive for the future. Omission of such undertakings from this list does not lessen their achievements, nor should it suggest their disqualification from a "Hall of Fame" for Russian-American success stories of the 1990s. There is simply not room to include them all in this limited presentation.[2]

FINDING AN IMMEDIATE NICHE IN THE RUSSIAN MARKET

Hundreds of American companies have tried to follow in the footsteps of Pepsi-Cola, McDonald's, and Mars in penetrating the Russian market.

Construction companies, cosmetics distributors, casinos, and Amway are among those firms searching for the nouveaux riches of Russia who have been smitten with Western comforts and consumer goods.

The forays of several technology-based companies offer interesting accounts of bringing modern and reliable products to a marketplace littered with low-quality and sometimes downright shabby items. The common thread among the following four examples is that each is serving a market niche evident even to the most casual visitor to the country.

RESTARTING THE ELEVATORS

In recent years, distraught passengers have been trapped in faulty elevators more than a hundred times per day in Moscow alone, according to the local press, with recovery times ranging from thirty minutes to several hours. The need for reliable elevators increases daily as aging, creaking cabins become less and less dependable. Meanwhile, construction crews install new elevators of various vintages in still more multistory buildings in their never-ending race to keep pace with the cries and complaints of cramped families and expanding commercial firms in cities and towns throughout the country.

Otis Elevator has entered into a number of joint ventures with Russian manufacturing and service organizations to upgrade elevator services in several cities, and these activities have employed hundreds of Russian engineers. Elevators in new office buildings proudly display the Otis label. And when the maintenance man from the firm Moslift appears with an Otis patch on his coveralls, anxious foreigners and seasoned Russians waiting for their friends to emerge from behind jammed doors breathe more easily.[3]

PROVIDING A CLOSE SHAVE

Shaving with a dull razor is not pleasant. Shaving with cold water is uncomfortable. Shaving with a dull razor in cold water is nearly impossible. The Gillette Company is determined to solve one-half of this problem, using advanced technology that has been successful in the United States. Since 1993, Gillette has manufactured blades and razors in St. Petersburg under its Russian joint venture, Petersburg Products International (PPI). Gillette owns 65 percent of PPI and has management control; a leading Russian manufacturer, Leninets, owns the remaining 35 percent.

The blade market in the former Soviet Union is estimated to be the third-largest in the world after India and the United States, and PPI is currently the leader in terms of market share by value. In July 1996, Gillette announced that PPI had acquired 100 percent of the blade and razor assets and trademarks of the St. Petersburg-based Factory for Consumer Products, a leading blade manufacturer in Russia that makes primarily double-edge blades under the Sputnik brand name.

PPI sells other Gillette wet shaving products as well as pre- and post-shave products throughout Russia. Gillette International LLC is also marketing electric shavers and nonshaving items in the country.[4]

ENTERING THE ELECTRONICS AGE

As suburban areas around many large cities bulge with rich Russians enjoying life in their new brick houses, the mobile telephone has increasingly become a necessity, or at least a symbol of modernity. For Russian children—rich and poor—electronic gadgets are "really cool." And with the increased incidence of crime, the demand for security alarm systems for cars and apartments seems unlimited.

Perhaps domestic manufacturers will eventually capitalize on this market, but at present they are all plagued with the Made-in-Russia label, an identification long equated with inferior quality in the electronics field. Thus, Radio Shack with its foreign-made goods has established a booming presence on Leninskiy Prospekt in Moscow. The products look strikingly similar to those in Radio Shack's American outlets.

While the magic of the most advanced electronic wizardry in its many forms may have arrived in Russia, for the present time Radio Shack apparently relies for its core business on the love of Moscow residents, transplanted from the Caucasus region in particular, for standard boom boxes, television sets, and headphones. At the same time, it reaches out to other Muscovite pocketbooks through displays of last year's computer models on sale and its catalogue of the latest items available from the United States.[5]

A PC IN EVERY OFFICE

Despite economic difficulties, the number of personal computers available to businesses and to individuals has increased dramatically. Very few of the computers purchased are of Russian design. Beginning in the late 1980s, an American investor and a Russian entrepreneur recognized this burgeoning market as a principal target for their new joint venture, Dialog, which features imported computers. Within five years, Dialog had sold and serviced more than one-half of the personal computers installed in regions where it was active.

The Russian partner, retaining wide authority over operations, has been considered the key to the venture's success. Time and again he has plunged the company into new businesses when such supplementary activities were necessary to circumvent supply breakdowns in Russia. Within several years, the company had acquired a bank, a construction company, an auditing firm, a securities brokerage house, and a stock exchange. This philosophy reflects the practice of many Soviet factories in years past: do it yourself to cope with shortages.

The American investor credits success to the skills of the Russian partner as a leader and decisionmaker. The Russian, in turn, credits the investor for giving him the freedom to act. Both have concluded that in searching for a partner the prospective entrepreneur should also look for a trusted friend. The Russian is now one of the leading commercial figures in the country. And his company proudly proclaims that it is the official representative of the Apple Computer Company in Russia.[6]

A Long-Term Perspective for the Russian Market

A number of companies, including the ones previously mentioned, are looking at the Russian marketplace from a long-term perspective, more concerned about establishing a solid presence than in earning immediate returns. Of course, these companies hope to operate on the black side of the ledger from the beginning, but they are primarily interested in having operations that provide a substantial profit stream over a period of a decade or longer.

Hundreds of American companies have professed to be involved in Russia for the long haul. The attractions of Russia have intrigued American company executives for decades. Yet only a few have been prepared to invest their own funds beyond occasional transoceanic visits and the establishment of local representation offices in Moscow. Several technology-oriented companies, however, have made major commitments to Russia, both in terms of buying and selling products and of bringing in advanced technologies.

Developing the Petrochemical Industry

Since the 1920s, Occidental Petroleum Company and its predecessors have maintained a presence in the country. Initially it was known for investments in fertilizer plants, but one of the company's most recent ventures has been in developing and exploiting oil fields in northwestern Siberia. Like other companies, it is having problems with the constantly changing Russian tax laws; it nevertheless expects to continue operations on a profitable basis.

The legendary Armand Hammer, former chairman of the company, was driven in his entrepreneurial efforts in Russia by his early encounters with Lenin and by his love for Russian art. Also, he personally arranged for American bone marrow surgeons to fly to Russia immediately following the Chernobyl accident. And, as many foreign visitors to Moscow quickly learn, he was the founder of the first combination hotel and international trade center in the city more than two decades ago.[7]

PROVIDING CHEMICAL PRODUCTS

For many years, Monsanto Company supplied a variety of chemicals to the Soviet Union, such as chemicals for rubber products, herbicides, and resins. Then Monsanto sold licenses for turnkey plants, providing technical advisers to help with construction and the initiation of operations at the plant sites. Later, the company became involved in introducing new technologies to the country, including processes for phosphate production to be used in chicken feed and for diamond-like coatings for sunglasses.

In recent years, Monsanto has also entered into several R&D collaborations with Russian institutions in plant genetics, polymer chemistry, superhard coatings, and pharmaceuticals. Supplementing these interests, Monsanto has equipped and staffed several research laboratories at the Moscow Institute of Bio-organic Chemistry. These laboratories provided a much-needed boost to the institute at a time when staff was leaving, equipment was becoming out of date, and paychecks were delayed for many months.

For the remainder of the 1990s, the company anticipates that business will be significantly below the level of 1991 because of the economic slump in Russia. Nevertheless, Monsanto plans to seek out new business opportunities and to remain a strong presence in the country.

Countertrade, or barter, has often replaced hard currency as a method of payment. Some companies engaged in the practice have complained that Russian goods may be of poor quality and that the same goods may have been earmarked for more than one Western partner. Monsanto's experience, however, has been very different. Russians have been tough bargainers in countertrade, but after they reach agreement, they provide goods that meet international standards while fulfilling the terms of the contracts.[8]

SEEKING A PLACE IN THE AEROSPACE INDUSTRY

The Boeing Company supports several private ventures in Russia and is the prime contractor to NASA for a major component of the international space station, which depends on participation by a variety of Russian institutions. Of course, the large market that will inevitably develop during the next decade for Western aircraft in the former Soviet Union is a major draw for the company. The fleet of Soviet-era planes serving Aeroflot and its spinoff companies is in poor repair, and, despite financial problems, domestic airlines are purchasing or leasing Western planes. Meanwhile, Russian production facilities are largely idle, with the quality of their workforces and equipment slipping further behind world levels each year.

To strengthen its standing within the Russian technical community, Boeing established a research facility in the center of Moscow in 1993. Relying on contracts with a number of Russian institutions and making use of the large pool of highly qualified Russian mathematicians and other scientists, Boeing has emphasized at this new facility development of mathematical algorithms and other projects of direct interest to its researchers in Seattle. The Russian specialists remain affiliated with their own institutions while carrying out research at Boeing. The center provides Boeing with access to a broad cross section of the Russian technical community that might otherwise be lured by the company's competitors from the United States and Europe. Also, it provides an impressive public relations backdrop for meetings with leading Russian officials.[9]

THE SOFT SELL FOR COMPUTER HARDWARE

For a number of years, Digital Equipment Corporation (DEC) has provided computer hardware and services to the Russian banking system and has explored other areas of interest in the country. Despite its recent financial difficulties and setbacks in other parts of the world, it has continued to look for new opportunities in Russia.

In addition to its sales of goods and services, DEC has sponsored experimental activities at many universities and research institutes in Russia. The company has provided free hardware and software to individuals or to departments to support research and education, assuming that this approach of seeding the academic market will eventually lead to large sales. This activity has often been likened to the efforts of Apple Computer Company in the United States one decade ago, when that company began to seek popularity among students through donations of its computers.[10]

CONVERSION OF RUSSIAN WEAPONS SCIENCE TO PEACEFUL PURSUITS

As noted in the previous chapter, the International Science and Technology Center (ISTC) in Moscow was established to provide financial support for former Soviet weapons scientists and engineers who are interested in switching careers. Other U.S. government programs also are targeted on helping weapons specialists adjust to new professions and contribute directly to the objective of preventing a weapons-related brain drain to countries of concern with regard to proliferation. Hundreds of projects are now under way as a result of these efforts. There is no doubt that as long as such projects are in progress, weapons specialists who are engaged will have little interest in looking to rogue countries for new challenges and fat paychecks.

However, the long-term viability of these programs, which were given funding for only two or three years, has always been a concern. In 1992 when U.S. dollars were initially made available, a common belief in Washington was that the Russian government would soon be in a position to take over the financial burden for continuing those projects that supported its own missions. Also, it was thought that Russian industrial firms would become interested in paying to use the results of the research activities in their manufacturing. Few Russian government agencies or industrial enterprises, however, are now in better positions than they were in 1992, and the likelihood of local financing for projects initiated with U.S. appropriations does not seem high.

TRANSMUTATION OF PLUTONIUM AND RADIOACTIVE WASTE

The project called Feasibility Study of Technologies for Accelerator Based Conversion of Military Plutonium and Long-Lived Radioactive Waste is the largest supported by ISTC—$3.1 million over a two-year period. Six Russian institutions that played active roles in the development of the Soviet nuclear weapons capability lead the project, with minor involvement by another half-dozen military-related institutes. More than four hundred former Soviet weapons scientists are participating, together with another three hundred scientists from the civilian sector.

The activity is directly linked to a still larger undertaking of the Los Alamos National Laboratory, and the Russian scientists look to Los Alamos to distribute the responsibility for the research components among participating laboratories from several countries.

Initially there was considerable skepticism among Russian and American officials in Moscow as to whether this project—with a very long-term payoff at best—warranted such a high level of support. However, the research team has made good progress in documenting the details of the most promising techniques for destroying plutonium while minimizing ecological damage. Meanwhile, interest in methods for safe disposal of excess plutonium recovered from surplus nuclear weapons has risen to the top of the international security agenda; in principle, the research should be of even greater political interest today than earlier.

It seems highly unlikely that Moscow will be prepared to provide significant financing to maintain Russian participation in the research group, and the United States probably will not again fund such an expensive project of the ISTC. While the weapons skills of the participants are a little rustier than they were two years ago, they still represent precisely the type of proliferation threat that the various programs discussed were designed to prevent. Just who will provide the funding for continuation long term remains a critical question.[11]

FROM CRUISE MISSILES TO EARTHQUAKE PREDICTION

Another ISTC project supported by the United States links Russian mathematicians, who designed the surface tracking programs for cruise missiles, with civilian mathematicians who have studied the subsurface behavior of seismic disturbances. Early concerns in Russia and the United States over the matching of skills between the two groups quickly disappeared; the teams are working together very effectively in improving the science of earthquake prediction. In particular, the cruise missile specialists have impressive computer skills that complement the theoretical expertise of their civilian colleagues.

In addition to keeping the former weapons researchers gainfully employed, the project offers the side benefit of desperately needed financial assistance for the collaborating civilian institute, which had fallen on very difficult times. Indeed, according to the leader of the project, without the three-year grant, some of the best scientists at the institute probably would have left for nonscientific pursuits.

Prospects for follow-on support after the three-year project comes to an end are not bright. Earthquake prediction is a research area that is usually supported only by governments, and the Russian government is unlikely to provide the money necessary for the teams to continue their efforts. At the same time, increased Chinese interest in cruise missiles—and in the scientific resources of Russia—has raised a few eyebrows both in Moscow and Washington. Again, follow-on funding will determine whether this project has been merely a Band-Aid attempt at combating nonproliferation or whether it will indeed result in fewer footloose missile guidance experts.[12]

BAR CODING OF NUCLEAR MATERIAL

In a project involving the U.S. Department of Energy, Russian security specialists at a research center in Obninsk, who had previously been involved in investigating the fissionable materials needed for nuclear weapons, are developing a new technology for safeguarding plutonium and uranium that has attracted media attention. Bar code scanners, similar to devices used in American grocery stores, scan labels that have been placed on tens of thousands of small containers of uranium and plutonium. After viewing a label, the device then scans a pad containing codes that indicate where the container is located, whether the container is being moved, and who is being given access to the container. The images are fed directly into a computer system, which maintains an inventory of the whereabouts of every container and the person responsible for each container, thus providing assurance that no dangerous material is missing.

The Russian specialists are proud to be associated with this modern technique, which has replaced handwritten notebooks in controlling tons of dangerous materials. Even if the bilateral support of the project should be terminated, Russian interests in safeguarding plutonium and uranium will remain high. Presumably, the Russian specialists, in spite of their meager salaries, will carry on with the system which is in place and operating; indeed, they may even attempt to replicate the technology at facilities in other cities as well.[13]

USING RUSSIAN TALENT AND TECHNOLOGIES
FOR U.S. PROGRAMS

After decades of trying to prevent the flow of advanced technologies from the United States to the Soviet Union, many U.S. government agencies are now strongly encouraging American firms to turn the tables and use sophisticated Russian technologies to achieve their own commercial objectives. Of course, many Russian politicians and officials are convinced that American firms are attempting to "cherry pick" selected technologies, with little concern over longer-term efforts that enable both countries to capitalize on such technologies.

Despite the wide publicity accompanying a few technologies that have captured the American imagination, there are few examples of Soviet/Russian technologies that have outstripped competing technologies for commercial markets. In almost every successful case, a Western company has been involved in the marketing of the technology.

REFINING THE ARCHITECTURE OF COMPUTER SYSTEMS

One of the early explorers of potentially useful Russian technologies was Sun Microsystems. Sun currently maintains research contracts with a Russian company, MCST, where about 250 specialists work on software projects and processor development. Despite the competing lure of non-technical jobs in Moscow, the leader of the Russian team has been able to maintain intact research groups that had worked together for many years. The researchers benefit both financially and technically from opportunities to work with Sun and other Western companies. In many cases, the flow of technical innovation has been from the Russian specialists to their Western partners, although many aspects of developing and marketing a successful software product are still being learned by the Russian partners.

Sun's interest in a relationship with MCST stemmed from a demonstration by the leader of the Russian team as to how technology developed for the Russian Elbrus supercomputer could be adapted for use in Sun's hardware. In short, he had done his homework. The cost to Sun of funding this kind of research project was relatively small.

One of the most important reasons for the initial success of the software projects was that within one year of start-up the Russians were able to deliver products that could be shipped to customers. After four years of collaboration, software is now completely developed and maintained in Russia. The Russian participants have clearly learned that customer satisfaction with the quality and time to market are critical in this type of venture. And, underpinning the technical considerations, the fundamental commitment to succeed despite logistical or other problems has been essential.[14]

PLASMA THRUSTERS FOR STABILIZING COMMUNICATION SATELLITES

For many years, American space engineers believed that plasma thrusters used for stabilizing communication satellites could significantly reduce their launch requirements since the weight of the payloads would be less, but such a system was never made operational. In Russia, however, a thruster of simple, rugged design had flown routinely on satellites for twenty years. Thus, when the technology came out from behind classified doors, largely through the effort of an American technology broker, Kiser Research, several U.S. companies became interested in acquiring it.

Because of large differences in design and testing philosophy between Russian and Western spacecraft, the Russians needed investors to help qualify their product under Western standards; they needed to protect their intellectual property; and they needed help in marketing the thruster in the West. An American company, Loral Space Communications, became interested, knowing that it would have to develop a new power processor and adapt the thruster for use in Western spacecraft. A joint venture was formed involving Loral, the Russian thruster manufacturer, and the associated Russian research institute. The joint venture, with the assistance of selected American and French firms, then began the process of marketing the product in the United States and Europe. While all signs are promising, several years will be required before sales of the thruster technology can be demonstrated.

Loral has identified four elements essential to successful establishment of a joint venture: *time* to build mutual confidence, obtain governmental approvals, and complete negotiations; *patience* in overcoming communications and regulatory hurdles; *money* to pay for travel and to keep the Russian partners from going bankrupt; and *courage* to take financial risks amid political and economic turbulence.[15]

MAINTAINING RUSSIAN BASIC SCIENCE

Despite the many calls beginning in 1992 to save Russian science, American funds made available for supporting basic science have fallen far short of the expectations of American proponents of strong U.S. action. These advocates were largely academics with colleagues working in the civilian sector of Soviet science—primarily in the institutes of the Russian Academy of Sciences and in several leading Russian universities. Their arguments did not persuade Washington in the way that others had successfully enlisted its support for diverting Russian military science to peaceful pursuits, for helping applied scientists commercialize their work, and for enabling ecologists to promote preservation of the environment.Their case for supporting basic science was less direct, and therefore it was more difficult to convince government agencies, concerned with Russia's immediate needs, to push civilian research with long-term payoffs at best to a higher priority. Despite warnings of a massive brain drain abroad, there has been no evidence of such a development. Claims that the basic scientists would follow in the footsteps of Sakharov to become strong forces for democratization could not be demonstrated in practice. Assertions that important research could be carried out in Russian laboratories too often were muffled by the dust of inoperative facilities. It soon became clear that the technical proficiency of Russian science in the 1990s would be well below the level of Soviet science in the 1980s, regardless of steps taken by Western countries; the U.S. government's reaction was to concentrate its largest programs on weapons scientists.

Nevertheless, the synergy between research and education as well as the long-term importance for the country of an infrastructure upholding basic research were recognized by some funding institutions. Also, pockets of research excellence survived for the time being. Thus, a few American programs were launched to encourage and support some of the remaining scientific oases in the country. As noted in the previous chapter, the largest efforts have been those supported by the International Science Foundation (ISF) established by George Soros, the National Science Foundation (NSF), the National Institutes of Health, and the Howard Hughes Medical Institute.

RUSSIAN ATTENDANCE AT INTERNATIONAL SCIENTIFIC MEETINGS

The termination of subscriptions to Western journals by Russian institutions, the lack of international travel funds, and the cancellation of most scientific conferences that had been held in Russia made the isolation of Russian scientists from world developments apparent to all. Without access to recent findings abroad, many Russian researchers foundered in their efforts to carry out studies supportive of international collaboration in fast-moving fields.

The ISF instituted a short-term Conference Travel Grant Program to address the problems associated with researchers' inability to maintain international contacts. During 1994 alone, it supported almost four thousand Russian scientists who attended close to a thousand conferences primarily in the United States and Western Europe but also in other parts of the world. With such a large program, the ISF was able to make special arrangements with Aeroflot to reduce travel costs, particularly in those cases that involved last-minute uncertainties concerning the issuance of visas. The program was targeted to basic research; it explicitly excluded from participation researchers in military-related and conversion projects and in the areas of applied science, the humanities, and the social sciences.

Conference attendance served several purposes. The Russian participants were able to catch up on happenings in other countries. Also, they presented information about their work that was not available either within Russia or elsewhere as a result of publication problems in their own country. Finally, useful contacts were made during these conferences, which led to development of cooperative projects and sustained communication by electronic means.[16]

INITIATIVES OF THE AMERICAN PHYSICISTS

When average salaries of Russian researchers slipped to less than $25 per month in 1992, American physicists were among the first Western scientists to take action. With the ISTC responding to the plight of the weapons physicists, the American Physical Society (APS) turned its attention to their civilian counterparts. The APS successfully raised funds from a variety of sources: its members, the NSF, the Soros Humanitarian Foundations and the ISF, and several other private foundations. With more than $1.5 million in hand, the APS was able to organize (a) programs of emergency grants to sustain colleagues until other sources of funding became available, (b) travel grants for attendance at major meetings, (c) support for summer and winter schools on various aspects of physics in Russia, and (d) grants of small equipment and parts. Also of importance was APS distribution of journals, initially funded by the NSF and then taken over by the ISF.

The APS also played a supporting role in the establishment of ISF programs that drew on the society's experience in transferring money to Russian scientists. The efforts of the American physicists have obviously paid off as large portions of the funds available for Russia through the ISF, the ISTC, the Department of Energy, the Department of Defense, and NASA have ended up in the hands of Russian physicists. The aggressive promotion of APS programs by influential American physicists who had long-standing ties with Russian colleagues and the deft use of international networks among physicists to provide up-to-date information on the evolving situation in Russia were important reasons why the pleas of American physicists were followed up with action on the financial front.[17]

SUPPORTING RUSSIAN RESEARCHERS THROUGH GRANTS TO AMERICANS

For several years, the National Science Foundation has provided supplementary funds to American scientists with current NSF funding who propose to include Russian colleagues in their research projects. This mechanism is designed to minimize administrative procedures and expedite delivery of funds. Merit review of the applications for supplements is not necessary. From the scientific point of view, the American researcher's original project had already been reviewed and recommended for NSF support. That scientist needs only to make the case that the project would benefit from Russian participation, either through work of the Russian specialist in the United States or through the American's travel to Russia.

The supplements include support for international travel and related expenses, communications and publications expenses, and expendable research materials and supplies. A one-time supplement of up to $5,000 is available for small equipment and journal subscriptions, as appropriate, to help sustain the Russian researcher's capability to work on the project in Russia.[18]

LAB-TO-LAB COOPERATION IN CRYSTAL GROWTH

The laboratories of the Department of Energy have undertaken many basic research projects in concert with Russian institutions, initially called lab-to-lab programs. However, that terminology now also refers to joint projects concerning the protection of nuclear materials, arms control verification technologies, and assessments of new technologies.

One interesting lab-to-lab project involved crystal growth at Moscow State University. By bringing a key scientist from the university to Lawrence Livermore National Laboratory for two years, American researchers were able to combine unique Russian experience in this field with the capabilities of the large facilities in California for accelerating the growth of very large crystals important in laser-fusion energy experiments.[19]

PRESERVING, STANDARDIZING, AND UTILIZING RUSSIAN DATABASES

Early victims of the decline in research budgets in Russia were geophysical and biological databases and collections of biological specimens that had been assembled at great expense over many years. The facilities housing the data deteriorated very quickly, and the staffs responsible for maintaining them have lost their interest and the financial incentives to mount salvage operations. Many of these databases and collections are of broad international interest, particularly those that include information about global phenomena.

Some American researchers have undertaken efforts to retrieve information from Russian notebooks that are slowly yellowing with age. Others have assisted Russian scientists in moving from notebook habits to the electronic age by providing both computers and advice on storing and retrieving data. However, many major databases have yet to be seriously dealt with either by international efforts or by the Russians themselves. The likelihood increases that much of the existing information about conditions related to the Russian environment will never be used; in many cases it will be easier to collect new data, with appropriate reliability safeguards, than to attempt to retrieve the old data, which may suffer not only from inadequate quality control during collection but also from the absence of proper storage.

FLORAL COLLECTIONS OF RUSSIA

Several American agencies and private foundations have invested $1.5 million in the preservation of botanical collections at the Komarov Institute of Botany and the Vavilov Institute of Plants in St. Petersburg. These funds have been used to refurbish greenhouses, heating systems, and related facilities. While much larger investments are needed in the future, this has been an important stopgap measure at two world-renowned institutions.

Convincing American funders to support this type of effort was not easy, even with the avowed commitment to biodiversity by government agencies and private foundations. Only through the perseverance of a single American scientist over a period of several years did funds finally become available to assist the institutions.[20]

EXPLORATION OF THE OCEAN'S FISH RESOURCES

For many years the Soviet fishing fleet plied the oceans of the world (including the seas off the Pacific and New England coasts of the United States), often raising suspicions about possible intelligence missions. However, most of the ships were catching fish; they were also gathering large quantities of scientific data about the biological conditions of the oceans. These data are important both in improving understanding of the impact of the intensity of fishing on various seafood stocks and in unraveling the mystery of global warming through clues contained in the oceans.

In 1995, the U.S. National Fisheries Service entered into a small contract with the Russian Atlantic Fisheries Research Institute in Kaliningrad (ATLANTNIRO) to begin to recover, catalogue, and store data from the 1961–78 Russian fish catches and related research activities off the New England coast. ATLANTNIRO's computer database is being modeled on databases maintained at the Fisheries Service's laboratory in Woods Hole, Massachusetts. With the Russian data in hand, the Woods Hole laboratory should be in a greatly improved position to trace the population fluctuations of haddock, perch, cod, mackerel, and other species and to understand the interrelationships of ocean temperature, fishing activities, and overall environmental conditions. A similar arrangement concerning selected Pacific Ocean fisheries was made in May 1996 with the Russian Pacific Fisheries Research Institute in Vladivostok (TINRO).[21]

IMPROVING RUSSIAN HEALTH STATISTICS

In late 1995, the U.S. and Russian governments jointly published *Vital and Health Statistics: Russian Federation and United States, Selected Years 1980–1993*. This document provides standardized data, using internationally recognized definitions that can guide health planners and policymakers at all levels in addressing public health issues. The underlying numbers, assumptions, definitions, and analytical techniques were developed in a collaborative effort to ensure a reasonable degree of integrity as well as comparability of Russian data with U.S. data. From the viewpoint of Russian specialists, the publication was particularly timely; it enabled them to capture and present data that might otherwise have been pushed aside or overlooked at a time of declining staff resources.

This report revealed many trends concerning diseases and other health problems in Russia. Of special interest has been the rapid decline during recent years in the life expectancy of males, which by 1993 had dropped to fifty-nine years and was still on a downward slope. This development, combined with a declining birthrate, led to an unprecedented crossover: in 1993 the number of deaths exceeded the number of births, resulting in an actual decline in population.[22]

ATTRACTING FOREIGN OIL AND GAS COMPANIES

During recent years, Moscow has insisted that foreign companies interested in exploration and development of Russia's oil and gas fields must pay dearly for relevant local databases prior even to being allowed to enter bids for access to the energy-rich basins. Many foreign firms have been reluctant to pay the hefty price of admission, not knowing whether they had a reasonable chance of winning competitions or even if the stakes were worth winning. Now, as a substantial part of the Russian petroleum industry moves toward privatization, Russian organizations appear to be moving (albeit slowly) to a more normal, market-oriented approach to attracting foreign interest in natural resources.

To encourage this evolution, in 1993 the U.S. Geological Survey (USGS), with support from AID, initiated a joint project with the Russian State Committee on Geology (ROSKOMNEDRA) to develop and make available to foreign companies regional-scale data sets on Russian petroleum geology. As part of the project, the USGS established technical facilities at seven ROSKOMNEDRA research institutes in Moscow, St. Petersburg, and Tyumen (western Siberia). These facilities include laboratories for seismic processing, petroleum geochemistry, and computer mapping. The information that is released as a result of the joint efforts will include regional seismic profiles, geochemical information on oil deposits and source rocks, and various databases characterizing the historical performance of Russia's petroleum basins. Regional data sets such as these have been commonly available at low cost for other regions but until recently have not been prepared for Russia. The goal of the program is to demonstrate to both the Russian government and the emerging private sector that making such regional-scale data products readily accessible will eventually stimulate Western investment and benefit the Russian economy.[23]

PROMOTING OTHER INTERESTS OF U.S. GOVERNMENT AGENCIES

The interests of many of the technical agencies of the U.S. government span a tremendous range—protecting natural resources and the environment, controlling diseases, exploring outer space, and ensuring order in worldwide transportation and communication networks. Their cooperation with counterparts in Russia goes back many decades, but increasingly this cooperation hinges on the availability of funds, in both Russia and the United States.

Unfortunately, on occasion too many senior U.S. officials making orientation visits accompany the specialists from the agencies on technical delegations. Conversely, the quest for per diem allowances has brought many Russian officials to the United States on missions of marginal importance, officials as interested in dresses for their wives or belts for their husbands as ideas for their agencies. Overall, however, the experts intent on solving concrete technical problems greatly outnumber the accompanying members of exchange delegations.

Continued interactions by representatives of the technical agencies of the two countries, handled properly, are very important. Some examples of the benefits deriving from several collaborations that have emphasized the technical aspects of joint enterprises are instructive.

TOGETHER FLYING HIGH

While the drama of the first Apollo-Soyuz rendezvous in space in 1975 may never be repeated, the recent resumption of outer space linkups continues to have political repercussions as well as to serve the financial interests of NASA and the Russian Space Agency. The experience of Russia in human space flight is unrivaled. For that reason, the bilateral agreement for carrying out U.S. shuttle flights to the Russian Mir space station is important in its own right. Moreover, the Shuttle-Mir program is vital to the international space station mission.

Shuttle flights are providing opportunities for life science and other experiments by American astronauts and Russian cosmonauts that lay the groundwork for the construction and use of the space station. The Russians are eventually to provide a number of components (see Appendix C for specifics). The technological advantages of Russian involvement are substantial: the station is considerably larger and its projected completion date much earlier than would be the case without Russian participation.

Some skeptics do not believe that the international space station will be ready for operation by 2002 as scheduled. Can political support be sustained in the United States? Will Russia have the resources to contribute its share? Will other foreign partners deliver their components as promised? And will Russian space technology continue to perform as in the past despite the continued slippage in the work habits of production personnel throughout the country? Whether or not the space station becomes a reality, the U.S. investment in joint experiments on Mir should help ensure that vast Russian experience is conveyed to U.S. and to other beneficiaries while at the same time Russian counterparts prosper enormously from the Russian-American partnership. Given the political and financial uncertainties in Russia, using this window of opportunity for intensive cooperation seems prudent indeed.[24]

LEADING THE RUSSIANS TO THE INTERNATIONAL NEGOTIATING TABLE

During the late 1980s and early 1990s, Russian specialists were active participants in the international dialogues concerning global climate change. They are now parties to the Montreal Protocol designed to reduce depletion of stratospheric ozone and to the international treaty on global climate change. This did not happen by accident; indeed, American specialists can take considerable credit for having encouraged Russia to take this topic seriously.

A bilateral working group—under of the U.S.-Soviet and later the U.S.-Russian Environmental Agreement—has spent many years debating the issues related to ozone depletion and global climate change and reviewing relevant research in the two countries and elsewhere. At a critical time when the Russians had left the international negotiating scene because of the unwillingness of the international community to accept their scientific theories, they turned to U.S. specialists for a sympathetic ear, only to learn that the Americans sided with their critics from other countries at the international negotiating tables. After lengthy bilateral debates, the Russians finally returned to the table, and they since have become constructive partners in global efforts to understand the scientific basis for the dramatic environmental changes facing the world community.[25]

CONSERVING THE WILDLIFE OF RUSSIA AND THE UNITED STATES

American and Russian specialists together have achieved a remarkable degree of success in their attempts to study wildlife common to the two countries. For the past several years American and Russian biologists have placed satellite-linked transmitter collars on polar bears and walruses along the coasts of Alaska and Chukotka to better understand their migration and feeding habits. U.S. aircraft with mixed crews have conducted surveys of nesting geese and swans on Chukotka. Specialists from the two countries tag some two hundred snow geese each summer on Wrangel Island and observe many of them in Alaska as they make their way south in the fall. Also, in an attempt to discover the cause of the dramatic decline of spectacled eiders in Alaska, American biologists have conducted field studies in Yakutia, where the species is more abundant, observing nests, collecting blood samples, and implanting satellite-linked transmitters. Finally, a seabird working group based in Magadan and Anchorage coordinates rapid exchange of the results from studies of mutual interest while avoiding unnecessary duplication of effort. These efforts, operating with minimal budgets, have been strongly supported by the

U.S. Department of the Interior and the Smithsonian Institution, as well as by a half-dozen Russian institutions.[26]

RELAXING MILITARY SECURITY BARRIERS TO COOPERATION

Secrecy cloaked much of the scientific research activity of the Soviet Union, and the fingerprints of that policy remain evident in many places in Russia. Of course, American protection of military secrets has also been widespread. Several recent projects that seem to offer promise illustrate how specialists in the two countries have been able to overcome secrecy barriers in structuring cooperative projects.

LISTENING FOR THE TEMPERATURES OF THE ARCTIC OCEAN

In recent years, American oceanographers have begun to document correlations between the acoustic properties of sections of the oceans and the temperature gradients of the same regions, with significant implications for studies of global warming. Initial experiments in the Southern Hemisphere proved successful in this regard; now interest has turned to the Arctic Ocean, where temperature variations are even more significant in predicting and responding to changes in the atmosphere.

After extensive diplomatic negotiations, arrangements have been worked out to permit scientists from the two countries to make acoustic measurements in marine areas that are favorite habitats of submarines and other naval vessels—a project entitled Acoustic Thermometry of Ocean Climate. Listening devices that will regularly record the thumps of sound generators are being emplaced throughout the Arctic region. Measurements of the speed of deep ocean acoustic transmissions over basin-scale distances will make possible the derivation by association of water temperature.[27]

FROM BATTLEFIELDS TO AGRICULTURAL FIELDS

More than 120 million land mines prevent resettlement of agricultural lands in a dozen countries of the world—Bosnia, Afghanistan, Cambodia, Rwanda, and elsewhere. The techniques for detecting and clearing the mines, particularly plastic antipersonnel mines, are woefully inadequate as thousands of professional mine experts, farmers, and children probe the ground with picks and sticks. Both the United States and Russia have developed many types of mines and have also invested sizable resources in technologies for finding and removing them. Both countries have been concerned with booby traps tied to mines, and Russia recently has been involved in clearing mines in Chechnya.

The U.S. Department of Defense has taken the lead in releasing for humanitarian use many of the technologies that had been developed for mine clearance during wartime. The Russian Ministry of Defense has agreed, in principle, to cooperate with the Russian Academy of Sciences in freeing up previously classified technologies of its own for use in cooperative efforts between American and Russian specialists. The Russians are believed to have made substantial progress in developing a hand-held, ground-penetrating radar system, advanced metal detectors, and devices for sniffing explosive materials. While a venture combining the expertise from each side is just beginning, it could prove useful in tackling a very difficult technical problem.[28]

SPIES IN THE SKY FOR ENVIRONMENTAL ASSESSMENTS

A mixed U.S.-Russian group of intelligence and environmental specialists has begun to identify imagery from classified satellite programs that can be used for environmental assessments. While the details are still being worked out, it appears that photos and other types of images with very precise resolutions will be helpful in pinpointing environmental problems in the two countries. As a first step, the group has exchanged maps and materials describing petrochemical contamination over a multiyear period at a military facility in each country. Specialists from the two countries are assessing the utility of this information for future environmental site characterization and remediation efforts. Russian satellite imagery, when combined with American data, appears also to be useful in understanding conditions in the frozen reaches of the Arctic Ocean.[29]

FROM SUBMARINE STALKING TO ENVIRONMENTAL CLEANUPS

In 1993, McDermott, Inc., received a grant from the U.S. Trade and Development Agency to carry out a feasibility study of converting facilities at the Komsomolsk-na-Amur Shipyard, which had produced nuclear submarines, into a commercial supplier of ships and offshore oil and gas recovery equipment. This grant was based on four criteria: the project was a development priority of Russia, it had potential for significant exports of American products, financing for follow-on activities would be available and open to American firms, and there would be foreign competition for such work.

The study included consideration of other possible commercial products suitable for the shipyard. As one result, the McDermott company announced in early 1996 that the Japanese government had awarded to the company and its Japanese partner a $25 million contract to construct a liquid radioactive waste treatment plant at the shipyard. The barge-mounted facility is to be located near Vladivostok and will be capable of processing 7,000 cubic meters of low-level nuclear waste each year. Conversion opportunities at the shipyard had stalled for several years after the initial McDermott grant, as the development of offshore oil fields requiring platforms was repeatedly delayed. Finally, lengthy diplomatic and technical discussions led to an agreement on the system for extracting waste contaminants from water used in the submarine decommissioning and dismantling process. [30]

INNOVATIVE APPROACHES

Among the thousands of Russian-American projects that have been undertaken are many novel approaches to cooperation that have proved successful. Russia has become a testing ground for hybrids that emphasize Western enthusiasm and Russian ingenuity while submerging Western skepticism and Russian frustration.

Many Russian and American veterans in promoting cooperation scoff at new approaches, particularly those that are invented in the United States. Similarly, self-proclaimed Kremlinologists have been appalled by the odd notions that newcomers to the Russian scene brought with them when the World Bank, AID, and other organizations opened for business in Moscow. How could an American who does not speak Russian, cannot identify a portrait of Peter the Great, or is afraid to make a U-turn on the Garden Ring Road possibly come up with ideas that would be effective in Russia? Still, experimental ideas have been the watchword of many successes, underscoring the importance of Mikhail Gorbachev's call for "new thinking."

DESTROYING TONS OF CHEMICAL AGENTS
PRODUCED FOR WEAPONS SYSTEMS

An estimated forty thousand tons of chemical agents stored in Russia and ready for use in weapons systems are the legacy of the Soviet chemical warfare program. Organophosphate-based nerve agents—Sarin,

Soman, and VX—constitute 81 percent of the stockpile, with the balance being blister agents—Lewisite and mustard gas. These chemical agents are contained in projectiles, rocket warheads, bombs, spray devices, SCUD missile warheads, and bulk storage containers.[31]

Both the United States and Russia are committed to destroying their stocks of such chemicals as quickly as possible. But what type of technology can be used for destroying these weapons? Technologies being considered in the United States may not be appropriate in Russia since, unlike the U.S. stockpile, none of the Russian weapons are believed to contain explosive components such as busters, fuses, or rocket motors, which are stored separately. Also, Russian weapons were welded together, thereby ruling out the reverse assembly process used in the United States, where weapons were "press-fit" during assembly.

Initially, the Americans proposed that the Russians must use techniques familiar to the United States, particularly high-temperature incineration of the chemicals. But the Russians demurred. They believed that they could devise better and cheaper ways to eliminate chemicals, and their environmentalists objected to incineration. After extensive negotiations, the Americans agreed that the Russians should develop their own approach.

The Russians proposed to transform their nerve agents into a slurry. The slurry would then be encased in bituminous blocks, which would be buried. While there would be environmental concerns over the fate of the buried blocks, these were not as great as the air pollution hazards associated with incineration, so argued the Russian experts. The initial laboratory-scale experiments were carried out in the United States. The second phase was conducted in Saratov with analysis at Moscow State University. A joint peer-review committee examined the work and reached the conclusion that satisfactory destruction levels had been achieved. Thus, Russian innovations are sometimes very effective.[32]

A NEW THRUST FOR YOUNG INVESTIGATORS

The National Academy of Sciences has set apart as a priority area programs of bilateral cooperation among young post-doctoral scientists in multidisciplinary studies. Such programs, jointly sponsored with the Russian Academy of Sciences, have provided the opportunity for more than thirty-five specialists from each country to carry out field studies together in four separate programs: biodiversity, Arctic ecology, drinking water contamination, and forest preservation.

The American participants are selected on the basis of national competitions, with the process ensuring that the individuals bring a multidisciplinary character to the teams. The Russian Academy has more difficulty in organizing its teams since non-Academy institutions have the strongest capabilities in some fields. Initially, an Academy institute was simply assigned responsibility for the agreed topic; not surprisingly, almost all participants were selected from that institute, thereby defeating the multidisciplinary purpose of the program. However, when it became clear that the program was oriented as much toward policy as science, the Russian Academy regrouped and began organizing more broadly based teams (although these were still lacking in policy experience).

The program supports bilateral collaborations in the chosen topic areas over a period of only two years. However, these initial contacts have been sustained by many of the participants, and some should continue for many years. For the Americans, the principal benefit has been the opportunity to meet colleagues interested in working at remote sites in Russia. For the Russians, a major benefit has been exposure of narrowly focused specialists to the broader policy aspects of complex studies.[33]

CUSTOMIZED MANAGEMENT TRAINING FOR RUSSIAN SPECIALISTS

No theme has been more popular in foreign assistance programs for Russia than management training. Unfortunately, there is now a surplus of Russian graduates of management training programs who have nothing to manage. A major problem has been an unwavering conviction among many influential Americans that general purpose management training would be helpful to Russians, who purportedly know little about modern management methods within a market economy.

One management training effort financed by AID has avoided the pitfall of bringing Russians to the United States for training that may have little relevance to what they do when they return home. The independent Academy for Educational Development has sponsored a series of carefully customized training programs for groups of specialists from Russia and the other countries of the former Soviet Union. Success has derived from selecting trainees who are responsible at their workplaces for narrow technical fields and designing the training programs to include whatever is required for managing these specific activities. Often, the appropriate Russian participants are busy at home, and therefore the training must be compressed into several weeks. The emphasis is on interactions with Americans who are managing in similar areas. While the program may seem expensive in that each step must be carefully tailored to the needs of the Russians, the payoff can be substantial.[34]

Finding the Right Russian Partners

In 1992, the Institute for the USA and Canada in Moscow, using a catalog of Russian defense plants prepared by a joint U.S.-Russian committee, identified a number of Russian firms in search of American partners for conversion projects. The institute, in cooperation with Pepperdine University, which had received support from AID, arranged for senior personnel from several dozen firms to travel to the United States to advertise their wares. Unlike many similar missions that have involved minimum preparation by the Russian participants and very short periods in the United States, this project combined education and sales. The Russian entrepreneurs were carefully schooled by Russian and American specialists before and during the visits in the preparation of business plans to be presented to potential partners.

Almost one-half of the more than one hundred Russian participants have reportedly succeeded in locating American firms sufficiently interested in their products to begin serious negotiations for joint ventures. While many of these negotiations may prove to be false starts, a substantial number have already shown considerable market potential.[35]

Providing Equipment for Environmental Monitoring

AID has been most comfortable when providing American technical advisers assigned to design and oversee projects in Russia. It has been much less comfortable in turning over money to Russian organizations that may not meet AID standards of accountability. It has been ambivalent about making available commodities other than food and medical supplies, but its program to provide environmental monitoring equipment to Russian institutions has met a desperate need that should pay off very handsomely. Despite internal resistance, agency advocates have been able to assist Russian institutions in the fields of energy conservation and environmental protection. While legitimate questions have been raised about supplying energy-related equipment to Gazprom and other financially stable Russian institutions, enabling less well endowed institutions, particularly the analytical laboratories of local administrations, to conduct environmental monitoring seems to be a very sound policy. If environmental protection is to be a priority in Russia, then improved monitoring capabilities are essential. The equipment, valued at $30 million, will make a significant difference in a few regions, while pushing the country down the road toward reliance on modern monitoring methods.

The key to success of the program has been the quality of responses by Russian institutions to the AID solicitation for applications from those interested in receiving equipment. With a rich pool of persuasive applications, a joint panel of AID and Russian officials was able to select a number of recipients that have a high likelihood of putting the equipment to good use and taking care of it over the long run.[36]

THE DEVIL IS IN THE DETAILS

In Russia, a vast realm of uncertainty lies between the signing of an agreement for international cooperation and the achievement of tangible results from that cooperation. Examination of the details of specific projects is the best way—indeed, the only way—to begin to have a realistic appreciation of the return on investments in collaborative ventures. At the same time, there are many intangible results of projects—both good and bad—that will not be easily uncovered even through the closest scrutiny of project details.

As presidents, ministers, and other government officials change in each of the countries, the new leaders will want to celebrate their own signings in the Kremlin and the White House. Agreements are important. But as budgets tighten and political winds change direction, anticipated and actual project results will be the primary criteria for judging whether projects should be initiated, continued, or terminated.

CHAPTER 4

THE RUSSIAN PERSPECTIVE

Unfortunately, science is still hostage to politics. It is necessary for the government to regulate joint activities of American and Russian scientists and specialists.

Russian deputy minister for science and technology policy
February 1996

Cooperation has achieved far more than could be expected.

Russian science policy analyst
March 1996

RUSSIAN CYNICISM OVER UNFULFILLED PROMISES

Public statements by the Russian president, prime minister, and other senior officials regularly applaud cooperative efforts supported with American foreign assistance funds. The Russian press carries many government reports of successful joint scientific projects underwritten by many funding sources. Whether the official pronouncements about joint endeavors are carefully crafted diplomatic proclamations or extemporaneous remarks, they seem to reflect genuine appreciation for efforts of the U.S. government to guide Russia through the difficulties of a society in transition. Of course, those Russian individuals who are beneficiaries, financially or technically, of successful projects are invariably strong supporters, while many Russian participants in projects that were not so successful seem too polite to criticize American efforts to be helpful.

However, some influential Russians have become cynical about American "foreign assistance" and express their views openly. They apparently thought that the various components of foreign aid would simply be replacements for state subsidies, which were drying up. Others presumably started with unrealistic expectations, while still others are simply seeking a whipping boy for their economic frustrations. The comments of the critics have sometimes been pointed.

> At the Vancouver summit meeting, Clinton promised $40 billion dollars in aid from the Western countries, with 40 percent from the United States. But very little has arrived. So we have adjusted, and we no longer assume that the United States will be a major source of financial assistance. We now know that your foreign aid funds must support American organizations which provide advisory services rather than assist our institutions directly. Sometimes your advisers help, but generally we can do without them. Take the Nunn-Lugar programs, for example. Only $120 million, or 10 percent of the available money, has actually been spent in Russia. That represents 1 percent of our Ministry of Defense's 1996 budget available for disarmament activities. The Nunn-Lugar program is interesting but not that important.[1]

These were the comments in February 1996 before an audience in Washington by an astute Russian political analyst who is a consultant to noteworthy members of the Duma. Despite his pessimistic tone, he was very favorably disposed to close relations between Russia and the United States. He simply was facing up to reality as he saw it.

This attitude should have been no surprise to the Americans around the table, yet they were taken aback. They apparently had not paid sufficient attention even to the American press, which for several years had been replete with reports of Russian disenchantment with foreign aid. In early 1994, a front-page headline of the *Chicago Tribune* reported, "Russians Wary of U.S. Promises; West Failed to Deliver Billions in Aid." The paper then went on to note, "Americans risk looking like shifty used-car salesmen if they blow into Moscow with yet another glitzy package of programs that have little chance of being fulfilled." It concluded, "Millions of conservatives, communists, and nationalists, casting about for someone to blame for the profound economic crisis afflicting their country, have convinced themselves that the United States is actively trying to destroy Russia as part of a grand plan to plunder its vast natural resources."[2]

Speaking more directly to the perceived drawbacks of technical assistance, which has been at the core of many programs involving science and technology, Moscow newspapers have featured reports on the extravagant spending habits of high-priced Western consultants residing in four-star Moscow hotels. And many Russian scientists and engineers have vented their convictions that technical assistance approaches designed for the third world that have been put forward by the European Union and the United States as models for Russia should play no further role in their country.[3] A deputy prime minister who was responsible for Russian policies concerning foreign assistance has set forth the more reasoned views of most Russian experts, whether they be discussing financial shortfalls or the need for retooling a highly skilled workforce, as follows, "The government is prepared to follow the course of reform even without further outside help, but external assistance could play a vital role in facilitating Russia's transition to a market economy."[4] In Washington in early 1996, a group of prominent Russian economists presented to U.S. government officials and academic colleagues their analysis of the effectiveness of American technical aid to Russia. While they seemed supportive and appreciative of the publicly espoused objectives of American efforts to help the Russian economy, they spent much of their time repeating the complaints that have filled the press on both sides of the ocean. They were critical of the Russian administration of the bilateral aid programs, but they reserved most of their barbs for the United States, as indicated in this excerpt from their report:

- The influence of the Russian side on project selection is reduced to a minimum.

- Experts are most often selected without Russian counterparts being involved. A number of experts have been unqualified to provide assistance. The travel expenses for experts, sometimes amounting to one-third of the total budget, are excessive.

- Russian specialists have repeatedly identified cases wherein projects were too closely linked to the interests of specific firms, which, as a rule, win tenders and obtain contracts for the implementation of projects. This opens the possibility for unpublicized deals and corruption on the part of both Western firms and Russian recipients.

- On some occasions, data from projects related to research and evaluation of industries, including specific Russian plants, were given to particular corporations, which subsequently used this information in devising their own investment strategies for the Russian market.

- One of the substantial flaws of technical assistance programs is the excessive share for consulting services. It makes more sense to combine technical assistance with the provision of investment credits and loans with favorable conditions.

- Russian experts have been studying their economic problems since well before perestroika, and the so-called experts from abroad demonstrate poor understanding of the real problems facing Russia, as evidenced by their abstract recommendations.

- Similarly, in some American research-oriented aid projects, there were attempts to deliberately build in conclusions which are clearly not in Russia's interest. For example, the American report for a joint research project on development of the Russian electrical energy sector, which resulted from an agreement between Vice President Gore and Prime Minister Chernomyrdin, contained proposals on dismantling the first generation of nuclear power plants. From the Russian perspective, the possibilities for improving the plants and for substantially increasing their safety systems have not yet been exhausted.[5]

A press conference, convened by the Ministry for Atomic Energy in September 1995, to address "international cooperation," showed how unsubstantiated political rhetoric that is critical of U.S. policies can complicate cooperation. The ministry spokesman strongly condemned U.S. efforts to pressure Russia, along with China and Argentina, not to sell nuclear reactor components to Iran, arguing that the United States had already (years ago) equipped Iran with a nuclear capability and that the Russian equipment would be subject to international safeguards. He bashed American government support for the Westinghouse Company's proposal to upgrade the safety of a nuclear power station built to Russian specifications in the Czech Republic, a plan he regarded as totally unrealistic and unsafe. He contended that the United States had reneged on a U.S.-Russian agreement for American purchases of uranium from Russia. Finally, he assailed efforts by the United States to derail civilian reactor projects of the Russian ministry in Cuba and North Korea as attempts to prevent international competition in nuclear reactor markets. In making these assertions, the spokesman did not hesitate to distort U.S. positions on the issues, often using inappropriate and inflammatory language to make his points. And this was at a time when many American nuclear

research laboratories were carrying out highly successful projects throughout the complex of the ministry. At the same time, there was not a word on
the positive aspects of bilateral cooperation, which ministry officials
repeatedly trumpeted during private meetings with U.S. visitors.[6]

Despite these pessimistic reports from Moscow, the United States
remains the preferred overseas partner for most Russian scientific institutions. In particular, trips to the United States under the rubric of various assistance and exchange programs continue to be cherished as
unique experiences, often offering opportunities well beyond the original
intentions of the programmers. "I don't care if a week of lectures on the
American social security system is irrelevant to our situation in the closed
atomic cities. I have lots of time off to see the wonderful sights of the
United States and to buy presents for my wife," declared a research institute director visiting the United States in late 1995. At the same time,
though, recognizing that the lectures were not helpful, he had slipped
out of several sessions to make contacts with American scientists interested in activities at his institute; he planned to miss the concluding ses-
sion for the same purpose.[7] Nonetheless, the general enthusiasm in
Russia over the payoff from foreign assistance has clearly declined since
the early 1990s, when there was omnipresent anticipation of a steady
flow of dollars from America.

VIEWS OF PARTICIPANTS IN COOPERATIVE PROJECTS

The criticisms of technical assistance expressed by Russian politicians,
journalists, and economists carry considerable weight within Russia, particularly among the general population. Yet they can be very misleading.
It is particularly unfortunate that some influential Russian figures consider all interactions in science and technology to be "assistance."

In order to provide a broader range of Russian views of the impact of
Russian-American efforts in science and technology, including activities
financed through foreign assistance programs, a policy analyst from the
Russian Academy of Sciences with extensive knowledge of cooperative
activities carried out a structured survey of the private views of twenty
Russian specialists during the spring of 1996 in support of this study. He
interviewed deputy ministers, institute directors, other policy analysts,
and bench scientists. He selected specialists who were very familiar with
the work of civilian laboratories of Russia. His limited survey comple-
ments a more detailed analysis of bilateral cooperation involving Russian

military laboratories in the midst of conversion activities that was presented in an earlier book by the author.[8] The most significant findings in this survey follow.

IMPORTANCE OF COOPERATION

All respondents gave great weight to the importance of cooperation with American institutions. Whether discussing some of the 1,500 American firms doing business in Russia, the 128 bilateral projects financed by the Ministry of Science and Technology Policy, the 60 existing university-to-university agreements, or numerous other activities, the interviewees were very positive in their overall assessment of collaboration during the past three years. They noted that this was a time when foreign funds were vitally important in maintaining impoverished research groups.

Several stated that cooperation had achieved far more than could be expected. Others thought that cooperation had failed to live up to expectations in terms of the financial resources that were made available or the concrete results that had been achieved. All believed that there is a promising future for collaboration, although adjustments may be needed, particularly with regard to the channels through which financing is provided. Global multidisciplinary problems relating to environmental issues were most popularly cited as areas in which scientists were looking forward to further collaboration.

Singled out for accolades time and time again by both administrators and scientists was NASA, whose activities have penetrated a large number of Russian organizations. Also considered in a positive light were the projects of the International Science and Technology Center in Moscow and the nuclear-related programs of the Department of Energy. The International Research and Exchanges Board received considerable, favorable attention, particularly for its efforts to link American and Russian institutions through sizable grants.

Projects that were cited by institute directors as having particularly impressive results included joint investigations of volcanic activity on the Kamchatka Peninsula, research on radioactive contamination of the Arctic, and the international human genome program. Two very important areas that deserve greater attention on a cooperative basis, according to several respondents, are international terrorism, particularly nuclear terrorism, and the safe disposal of more than forty Russian submarines with active nuclear reactors that are scheduled for decommissioning.

Many respondents considered programs with the United States essential to balance the surge in cooperation with Western Europe, which can be reached using inexpensive train tickets, and with some countries of the Far East apparently ever-prepared to pay airfares and generous per diem allowances for Russian visitors. Also, some respondents believed that the United States and Russia were in a unique position jointly to lay out program strategies for addressing many of the most pressing global issues.

While respondents did not criticize specific American-sponsored projects, several did complain that, since Washington controlled most of the funds and Americans could therefore insist on designing programs their way, most of the projects were targeted toward issues that were of primary interest to the United States. Another common complaint by institute directors and scientists was directed at the false expectations raised concerning possible contracts for Russian institutions in support of the supercollider project developed by American physicists and later cancelled in Congress.

THE FINANCIAL CRISIS AND THE UNCERTAIN FUTURE OF RUSSIA

Political instability, economic chaos, and financial uncertainty within Russia were repeatedly mentioned as conditions that greatly complicate cooperation. A related concern was the inadequacy of the legal framework in Russia for carrying out any type of activity involving transfers of funds from abroad.

One researcher noted that talking about long-term cooperation made little sense when the participants in programs were struggling for day-to-day survival. Another stated that Russians could only participate in cooperative programs part time since they needed second jobs to make ends meet. Many others underscored the importance of cooperative projects with short-term results that could be used to fortify requests for additional funds to keep the research groups alive. Several predicted that, regardless of the country's political future, science and technology cooperation will continue to be an important contributor to raising the overall standard of living in the country.

The respondents reported that the lack of resources has caused almost all Russian scientific organizations to look to American or other foreign partners for financial help. In those cases where foreign support is limited, projects often suffer delays or fail completely. Having insufficient funds to pay for electronic communications, to sponsor participants in meetings about coordination, or to cover the costs of translating critical documents can quickly jeopardize project continuity, they emphasized. Even when funding for the Russian participants is relatively generous, the scientific team is dependent on the fate of the institute where it is housed. The institute directors emphasized that many institutions lack enough money to keep all their doors open, causing frequent disruptions of funded projects.

Reference was repeatedly made to the lack of opportunities for young scientists to travel abroad. The consensus was that such experiences could encourage young professionals to continue with scientific careers rather than to leave for the commercial sector. One institute director suggested that the Russian Academy of Sciences or some other organization make arrangements with Aeroflot to provide inexpensive airline tickets for Russian participants in cooperative projects even if they did not work within the Academy. Such discounted arrangements had been in place until the institutes became somewhat autonomous, and now airfares are so costly that many trips are simply cancelled.

OTHER CONCERNS REGARDING U.S. POLICIES

Negative comments from the survey centered on the difficulty in gaining access to some American research facilities under the control of government agencies such as the Department of Energy, the delays due to problems of paperwork and overseas shipment in acquiring equipment purchased in the United States, and the lack of timely information about procedures for applying for fellowships and grants from U.S. universities and foundations. Another issue on the minds of those contacted concerned snags in transferring funds to institutions in Russia at a time when uncertainty surrounded the security of both institutional and personal bank accounts. One suggestion was to use only an affiliate of an American bank in Russia or a highly reliable Russian bank offering procedures for payments without excessive fees. One further target of criticism was NASA's practice of using intermediary organizations to distribute its funds—a system that resulted in frequent delays.

Finally, the survey revealed a widespread belief that many important Russian programs are poorly known in the United States. Publications and other means were suggested for broadening the reach of information about Russian science to audiences abroad.

INTERNATIONAL COMMUNICATIONS

Some respondents singled out the Internet and the World Wide Web as important developments in which they would like to participate.

Others lamented the absence of modems and computers for access to electronic mail, noting that all such communications must go through institute directors. Some institutes still have difficulty with faxes, and the costs of telephone calls have increased dramatically. While all surveyed recognized the poor state of the telecommunications infrastructure in Russia, they looked forward to the day when e-mail would be routine.

In the meantime, frequent seminars can compensate for inadequate electronic communications. However, greater attention to learning English was repeatedly cited as important in this regard. In a related area, a new emphasis on distance learning was proposed, relying on new electronics technology to transmit educational programs on a worldwide basis.

THE GORE-CHERNOMYRDIN COMMISSION

The survey suggested that the Gore-Chernomyrdin Commission is somewhat of a paper tiger, praised by government officials but of seemingly little importance to researchers. It has brought high visibility to many science and technology activities, but more than political will is needed to implement projects. While the commission was felt to provide a good mechanism for focusing attention on important issues, it has no long-term strategy and little ability to resolve day-to-day problems. It has no funds to support implementation, and the tax and customs officials do not pay attention to its directives. Some respondents thought it was easier to persuade the commission to agree to a program than to convince the various bureaucrats involved in the process to implement it. Significantly little is known in Russia about how the commission works; therefore, many good ideas are never considered nor even presented. The commission was criticized for not "resolving" the issue of intellectual property rights, for sponsoring a poorly conducted study of Russia's energy needs, and for ignoring applied research issues.

Suggestions included establishing a small fund under the direct control of the commission, so that managers of new projects could meet to discuss steps for launching them, and organizing an advisory body to recommend long-term priority areas for collaboration. Several respondents urged the National Academy of Sciences to take the lead as it had in 1992 to mobilize the American scientific community, in consultation with Russian colleagues, to consider the future cooperation agenda. These views could then be presented to the Gore-Chernomyrdin Commission.

THE OFFICIAL RUSSIAN VIEW

In late March 1996, the author conducted an interview at the Russian Ministry of Foreign Affairs to obtain a more "official view" from a senior diplomat who was very familiar with the evolution of Russian-American cooperative endeavors, particularly in science and technology. In addition, on the following day, a Russian deputy minister at another ministry who is also heavily involved in cooperative programs offered his assessment. Both officials are well respected for their candor and willingness to discuss openly issues that are very difficult for the Russian government. Their views ran along largely similar lines:

- There are two courses of action regardless of the party in power in Russia: continuation of the current close Russian-American cooperation or a return to the confrontational stand that persisted during the cold war. Most leading Russians dismiss out of hand the second alternative. And few Russians consider that the relationship should have anything to do with foreign aid; both countries should benefit.

- Russia has become accustomed to reacting to initiatives from the United States, and the Russian government was disappointed that President Clinton would not offer new ideas at the G-7 summit to discuss nuclear-related issues in Moscow in April 1996.

- The Gore-Chernomyrdin Commission has been very valuable in promoting cooperation. It cannot solve all problems, but it can be very effective in identifying them and then designating appropriate agencies to try to find solutions. For example, the customs issue long inhibited cooperation in space exploration. At the insistence of the commission, the Foreign Ministry took the lead to obtain ratification by the Duma of an agreement granting a customs exemption for items shipped into Russia for use in cooperative space ventures. Perhaps the commission meetings should be less frequent, depending on the number of outstanding issues; but it is important that the United States and Russia—both great powers—meet regularly at a high level to address the practical aspects of joint programs. The Russian government considers the commission so successful that it has proposed a similar approach in its relationships with

France, Canada, and Brazil—perhaps at a slightly lower political level.

● With the impending termination of most American foreign assistance programs, U.S.-Russian relations are entering a new phase; new mechanisms will be needed to support cooperation. A special body should be established within the framework of the Gore-Chernomyrdin Commission to study alternatives and recommend new mechanisms. This is far preferable to reliance on the United States Congress—on its own, without benefit of prior consultation with Russia—to develop such a mechanism.

In summary, these very senior officials were enthusiastic—but pragmatic—supporters of expanded cooperation to be orchestrated at the highest levels of government.

In May 1996, two lower-level officials who were responsible at key ministries for overseeing implementation of bilateral projects, particularly those endorsed by the commission, released a barrage of complaints about the U.S. government during interviews in Moscow. To them, the essence of successful cooperation was resolution of problems associated with intellectual property rights, customs and tax requirements in Russia, timely issuance of visas, and access to government-controlled facilities in the two countries. According to their account, Washington wanted ownership of all intellectual property rights to be exploited outside Russia resulting from joint projects, expected across-the-board exemptions from the tax and customs laws of Russia, regularly requested last-minute changes in agreed participant lists, and insisted on access to sensitive Russian facilities without reciprocal access to similar facilities in the United States. While exaggerating the nature of U.S. positions, they clearly felt that Russia was giving up more than it should in each of these areas. Still, they considered the Gore-Chernomyrdin Commission to be very important and said that they were prepared to abide fully by the decisions reached on high.

There is no doubt that the official Russian view recognizes bilateral cooperation in science and technology with the United States as highly desirable and as deserving high priority. At the policy level, expanded cooperation provides a useful impetus to developing deeper and more fruitful relations between the two countries. But at the working level, cooperation is only meaningful when the many roadblocks to joint efforts can be successfully pushed aside. Unfortunately, this need for conflict resolution comes at a time when the very administrative staffs assigned to the details of implementation within the Russian government are being reduced.

LIFE OUTSIDE THE CAPITAL

We are in a very difficult period. Our staff has dwindled. Many of our young scientists are unwilling to work in a harsh climate for low salaries, even though they receive a 70 percent Siberian bonus. Our budget contains no funds for equipment or field work. Still, we are better off than most institutes in Eastern Siberia.[9]

These words in February 1996 of the director of the Institute of Biology of the North in Magadan, a city on the distant Pacific shore, underscored the importance of his mission to the United States to obtain additional external financing for maintaining the semblance of a research program at his isolated institute.

The financial support—in this case from the programs of Soros and the U.S. Fish and Wildlife Service—made up a very small percentage of his institute's budget. But it was an important ingredient. It allowed the institute to stay in contact with the outside world through an e-mail connection and occasional trips to Alaska. Perhaps of even greater significance, it demonstrated that someone really cared whether the institute survived, and it trained the staff in preparing research proposals that could be used as the institute searched for grants from other sources at home and abroad.

The Institute of Biology of the North had never expected to receive foreign assistance. Indeed, it does not like to consider research grants from abroad as assistance but rather as recognition of Russian contributions to solving problems of global interest. According to its director, those scientists who received grants were actually grateful to the United States. But those who did not were displeased with the disparities in salaries that characterized the institute as a result of the topping up of some paychecks by grants.

Two hours to the south of Moscow is Pushchino, where six biology-oriented research institutes and a new university are located. A visit to two of these institutes in April 1996 demonstrated the different ways in which institutions outside urban areas are responding to the financial crisis. Evidence of financial shortfalls was common in both institutes. Neither had electricity on the day of the visit. Both had many inactive laboratories. Many staff members were abroad. Those scientists that were present were older rather than younger.

But the program orientation and management approach of the two institutes were quite different. One institute had revamped its basic research profile almost entirely to confront near-term ecological problems since that would appeal to funding institutions, particularly those from abroad. The other institute clung to its tradition of pushing the furthest frontiers of science, confident that its unique contributions would be widely recognized and rewarded. The Institute of Soil Sciences, in applied ecology, succeeded in enticing back to Russia its many scientists who had traveled abroad, relying on promises of dachas and private agricultural plots that were under the control of the institute. The other organization, the Institute for Protein Research, lost a number of its best scientists to the brain drain. Its leaders rationalized these losses by contending that this international network of alumni would in the long run benefit the institute.

The applied ecology institute was casting its lot with the foreign assistance agencies and international agricultural and ecological funds. Its academic contacts included several small colleges in the United States that considered programs in Pushchino to be unique international experiments. The basic research institute was successful in attracting grants from the Howard Hughes Medical Institute to promote fundamental biomedical research. Its counterparts in the United States were primarily the large research universities, which have networks of collaborators around the world.

Beginning in late 1993, it seemed that every funding agency in the United States adopted the philosophy of locating more and more of its projects at sites remote from Moscow and St. Petersburg, in regions where dependence on and deference to central authorities was less pronounced. Of course, the scientists of Magadan and Pushchino welcomed this approach; in remote locations a little money can go a long way. If near-term political impact is the objective of a foreign project, siting it far from Moscow is a very good strategy.

MIXED REVIEWS FOR AMERICAN EFFORTS

A favorite joke in Moscow quotes a Russian official lamenting, "While the Americans never sent their armies to Russia, we are now facing a greater danger. Every day squads of Americans in three-piece suits set out from the Radisson Slavyanskaya Hotel, briefcases in hand, for institutions in every part of the city." Some conservatives in Russia accused the Soros foundations of supporting spies. These voices will continue to belittle the value to Russia of American contributions. Even Moscow's Mayor Yuri Luzhkov, whose coffers are overflowing with revenues from the city's financial dealings with the West, will continue to criticize unchecked foreign penetration of the city. Recently his administration unleashed a squad of painters skilled in the arts of the Cyrillic alphabet to counter the influx of English-language signs in the city.

At the same time, the Gore-Chernomyrdin Commission remains headline news as a symbol of hope and optimism, exemplified in an issue of *Finansoviye Izvestiya* in July 1996, "Gore and Chernomyrdin Sign Almost Thirty Documents and Promise a Jump in New Investments in Russia."[10] While it is easy for Russians to point out shortcomings of American initiatives in their country, they would have difficulty ignoring the many positive aspects. Beyond contentment with more cash in hand, many thoughtful scientists and engineers realize that their exposure to American ways has radically transformed the internal dynamics of science and engineering institutions throughout the country. Americans receive much of the credit for progress in Russia toward delegation of program authority from institute directors to project leaders, more honest accounting in the use of research funds, broader communications among research teams within Russia, and complete documentation of how experiments are conducted.

Russian officials, whether reformist or conservative, naturally will not turn their backs on the $10 billion package offered by the International Monetary Fund. Of course, smaller programs will have much more political difficulty meeting the tests of time. In the meantime, though, hundreds of Russian officials have become so accustomed to the new opportunities attendant on working with the Americans—which usually include personal benefits for themselves—that they will press for continuation. Most important, at the working level, tens of thousands of scientists and engineers, far removed from the purview of the naysayers, have pinned their hopes for survival on their participation in cooperative projects with American colleagues, and they will repeatedly boast about the results of these programs.

CHAPTER 5

AMERICAN PERCEPTIONS AND LESSONS LEARNED

*The Russian spirit is very strong, the young researchers are full of
enthusiasm, and their contributions to joint projects are manyfold.*
An American scientific exchange participant
September 1995

The Russians have an attitude problem.
Conservative staff member of the U.S. Congress
February 1996

POSITIVE APPRAISALS OF COOPERATION

The executive branch is always very positive about the progress that
has been made through bilateral programs with Russia, particularly
in technical areas such as space, nuclear, and environmental cooperation.
Indeed, never before has there been such a flood of optimistic announce-
ments, statements, and press releases by the offices of the president and
vice president as to the success of technical collaboration with a foreign
country. Of course, each of the two dozen U.S. government agencies
involved in working with Russian scientists also persuasively broadcasts
its own triumphs.

As would be expected, in reporting their experiences at conferences
and in press releases dozens of American organizations that have received
financial support from the many new government-financed programs
seem convinced that their activities have been important. Those organizations that have been unsuccessful in obtaining government funds
are less positive in their views; nevertheless many of them also believe
in the importance of the missions of their competitors. The General

89

Accounting Office, frequently an unstinting critic of shortcomings in the management of government programs, reports many successes in bilateral programs with Russia.

A few comments by recent American participants in joint research illustrate the specific benefits that can result from cooperation:

- A focused effort between Moscow State University and our university will dramatically enhance the level of results that we might otherwise obtain in each of the countries.

- Although Russian science in general is not as advanced as American approaches, there are unique ideas and approaches which will benefit the United States.

- Russians provide us with invaluable but previously inaccessible research specimens.

- Cooperation has produced new research directions.

- Our Russian visitor added significantly to research programs at our university.

- Our Russian visitor's work will form the basis for a Ph.D. thesis by one of our graduate students.

- The benchmarking software our Russian colleague produced during his visit is immediately useful.

- The cost of our colleague doing the work independently in Russia would have been many times greater.

- All of my Russian collaborators are extremely dedicated and reflect this dedication in our cooperative projects. They have to be dedicated, given the low level of pay.

- Our visitor has taken a laptop computer back to Siberia, where he will carry forth our joint work.

- The influence of senior Russian researchers is enhanced by Western exposure.

- There are a number of extremely bright, highly motivated scientists in Russia who have received no recognition outside the country.[1]

The personal interactions reflected in these comments are a particularly popular theme among U.S. congressional leaders, who generally support such exchanges. Since the 1950s, the intercultural experience has been a principal benefit of science and technology cooperation for important specialists of both countries. But congressional enthusiasm for spending on activities beyond people-to-people programs has been steadily declining.

A RELUCTANT CONGRESS

Within Congress, the initial euphoria over the demise of the USSR gradually gave way to disenchantment over the inability of the United States to guide effectively Russia's transition to an acceptable, Western-style political and economic model. While the Republican administration of George Bush led the efforts of the Western countries to engage Russia in cooperation at all levels, the Republican-dominated Congress of the mid-1990s has looked askance at the political behavior of the present Russian government and the limited effectiveness of American assistance programs in influencing it.

Some extremists in Washington believe that the Soviet Union was defeated by the West, and as a result the successor states—and particularly Russia—were obliged to sacrifice national sovereignty and even national pride in international dealings as they take their places alongside the remnants of other broken empires. Of course, no Russian leader worthy of his post would sit still for such a notion.

For several years, Washington critics of American support for President Yeltsin have railed at developments in Chechnya, at the perception of a latent desire of Russian conservatives to reabsorb Ukraine within a greater Russia, at Moscow's failure to meet obligations under several international arms control agreements, at the U-turns on Russia's road to economic reform, and at the rising tide of nationalism and communism throughout the country. Foreign assistance to Russia became the lightning rod around which the frustrations of these critics gathered.

It is not difficult to find soft spots in America's overall foreign assistance portfolio for Russia. Billions of dollars have been spent. Returns of comparable magnitude are hard to discern. Indeed, to some American critics, clear benefits to the United States have been meager. It is easy to lay at Russia's doorstep the blame for all shortcomings associated with this massive undertaking. Since we paid the piper, we should call the tune without Russia's interference, so runs the frequent complaint. Too few leaders of Congress are willing to take the time to look beyond such glib sound bites in making their evaluations.

From the outset, Congress has tied joint programs, including those in the fields of science and technology, with Russia's political behavior though the linkages have generally been subtle. The Clinton administration has attempted to insulate technical proceedings from political confrontation in Washington whenever possible, but it is very easy for American skeptics of a policy of active engagement to introduce constraints on assistance during the congressional appropriations process.

Of course, overarching the political concerns about Russia's aggressive role in the world and the costs of America's appearance to be intimately involved with the country's leaders during a delicate transition period are the more general congressional preoccupations with a balanced budget. The steady decline in public support for foreign assistance programs across the board does not help.

In short, important political circles in Washington do not believe that the investments of government dollars in Russia-oriented activities since 1991 have reaped so many benefits for the United States as to warrant future appropriations for programs of comparable size and scope. At the same time, some financial pipelines still contain unspent funds appropriated in earlier years, and the momentum among past program participants to continue cooperating is strong. Before the end of the decade, however, the U.S. government's financial commitment to Russia is slated to be very small.

In the absence of dramatic changes in both Washington and Moscow, "leave it to the private sector and the multinational financial institutions" may become the catchphrase in Washington. Private investment funds should replace government expenditures, say the guardians of the taxpayers' pocketbooks. Such a limited policy would be tragic. The private sector has an important role to play, and the programs of the World Bank and the International Monetary Fund are important for economic stabilization and for development of the country's physical infrastructure. But U.S. government programs involve leaders from many walks of Russian life and are extremely valuable in encouraging the evolution of a stable society that will continue to support American security, economic, and environmental interests.

Evolution of the Programs of AID

Among the harshest American criticisms of the U.S. government's role in Russia have been those leveled at AID. One of AID's principal thrusts has been the promotion of economic reform. When the AID-supported reformers lost favor with Yeltsin and with the Russian people, attacks on AID mounted accordingly.

Science and technology have been relatively minor components of the AID portfolio. Therefore, critiques concerning these areas are simply subsumed within broader reviews of the agency's performance. Despite many projects in environmental protection and energy conservation, even these have been perceived by some as fields of missed opportunity.

AID has seemed reluctant to consider seriously approaches proposed by outside groups in competition with schemes conceived by its own staff. This lack of outreach reduced the interest in AID's mission of a number of American scientific leaders who had much to contribute to programs in Russia and to the defense of foreign assistance on Capitol Hill.[2]

Nevertheless, AID has played important roles in the support of the technical work of Russian organizations. Programs gradually reached down to the grass roots. Many projects produced visible results, and the agency was frequently successful in leveraging funds from other sources, including the international development banks and the private sector. Still, a common view within the American and Russian science and technology communities has been that the payoff for AID in Russia was not commensurate with the investment.[3] Had AID devoted a larger share of its resources to more sharply focused science and technology programs that had potential multiplier effects in stimulating new types of economic development, the impact would have been much greater, they argue.

The Importance of the Cooperative Threat Reduction Program

Despite the national security rationale and focus of the Cooperative Threat Reduction (CTR) program, many American journalists and observers monitoring Russia have viewed it largely as another element of American economic aid to Russia. Indeed, the differences between building homes for retired military personnel pursuant to CTR and erecting houses for the general population as a component of economic assistance seem small to those who are not steeped in the intricacies of Russian and American laws. Conversion projects at Russian defense plants sponsored by the Defense Enterprise Fund are easily confused with similar ones supported by AID funds. Many American organizations have contracts both with the CTR and the AID programs. Thus, it is not surprising that CTR is often stained with the same brush that has yielded negative portraits of AID.

On close examination, however, the CTR program can claim a number of positive achievements. It has provided funds and equipment that facilitated the return to Russia of more than a thousand nuclear warheads from Ukraine, Kazakstan, and Belarus; helped remove to secure storage more than twenty-five hundred warheads from missile and bomber bases; and paved the way for elimination of several hundred missile launchers and bombers within Russia. The program has been an important catalyst in mobilizing funds from other sources, such as the Overseas Private Investment Corporation, to accelerate the conversion of defense facilities to civilian production. It has played a central role in Russia's retaining weapon scientists who might otherwise have scouted for funds offered by pariah states in search of weapons technologies.

However, delays during both the Bush and Clinton administrations in launching the program resulted in Congress withdrawing authority for use of some of the appropriated funds. Technical disagreements between Russian and American experts as to the best approaches for destroying chemical weapons and for long-term storage of plutonium pits removed from nuclear weapons extended the time horizon. Even after projects were fully agreed upon with Russian counterparts, cumbersome procurement requirements of the Department of Defense delayed the delivery of hardware overseas. Thus, until recently, when the administrative bumps in the road began to wear down, some vocal critics considered the CTR initiative a good concept that could not be translated into effective projects.

During this period of stutter starts, U.S. agencies realized the importance of pursuing multiple paths in establishing cooperative programs with military overtones. When formal diplomatic negotiations over upgrading security controls for nuclear material at the closed cities of the Russian defense complex broke down, the Department of Energy turned to its scientists, who followed the less formal lab-to-lab route and successfully initiated contacts that blossomed into major programs. When the U.S. government reached a stalemate on promoting government-to-government exchanges of researchers who were experts on biological agents that had been linked to warfare, the government again turned to the scientists to seek channels of freer interaction.

Now the programs are moving forward on many fronts. Perhaps of greatest importance has been the unprecedented degree of interaction between the national security establishments of the two countries—both civilian and military. While the true impact of such contacts is hard to measure, the leaders responsible for security on each side surely now understand one another better than at any other time in recent history.

STRATEGIES FOR TECHNOLOGY-ORIENTED FIRMS

After several years of probing, American firms have learned that uncertainty will remain as a way of life in Russia for the immediate future. There will be recurring, vexing questions concerning investment laws and regulations, tax changes, ownership rights, resolution of jurisdictional disputes, and currency convertibility. The lack of a Western business culture in Russia will also continue to plague outsiders.

One study of thirty-three joint ventures concluded that the most important ingredient for success is careful selection of Russian managers who are vested with broad authority. These managers should not only be able to direct operations effectively but should also be trustworthy and independent of underworld ties. Other principal findings were that, contrary to public perception, quality matters every bit as much to Russian customers as to Westerners and that success depends on a firm's ability to respond rapidly to problems arising from economic turbulence and social change.[4]

A related study noted that during recent years certain obstacles confronting joint ventures have become more problematic: the unstable economic environment, insufficient investment capital, and disagreements between venture partners. Other obstructions have diminished in importance: the lack of profit orientation among Russian counterparts in industry, the Communist mentality of workers, and insufficient attention to advertising.[5]

A third study emphasized the importance of a long-term presence in Russia. It suggested that Americans work directly with plant and institute directors, and not through intermediaries, to make deals and that they take pains to meet Russian business partners halfway. The pay-off from training in modern business practices, and particularly accounting and marketing, was highlighted. A final tip was to master U.S. and Russian security, export control, and customs regulations and procedures.[6]

PERSISTENT STUMBLING BLOCKS TO COOPERATION

Descriptions of the problems encountered in developing and carrying out science and technology programs in Russia could fill many volumes. They provide easy targets for those who are intent on challenging the value of cooperation. Two short lists may be helpful in appreciating the difficulty of operating at the project level and in explaining the slow pace of progress toward success.

The following official U.S. government list was prepared in 1993. Some of the difficulties have been overcome, but other observations still seem valid:

- Key Russian institutes are on the brink of collapse.

- Complexities abound in transferring funds to Russia, with taxes and other charges taking as much as 60 percent of the total.

- Administrative chaos and decentralization result in approvals and permits issued in Moscow not being recognized elsewhere, ministries requiring payments to middlemen, and payment procedures being inconsistent and unpredictable.

- Difficulties have arisen in finding effective Russian inter-locutors as previous ones have moved into more lucrative professions.

- Difficult conditions inhibit activities in the science cities.

- The lack of science management skills is pervasive.

- Overmanning in the science sector results in bloated projects.

- Brain drain takes away many of the best collaborators.

- The lack of international coordination, particularly with regard to information on Russian capabilities and on bilateral and multilateral programs, results in duplicative efforts.

- Export controls inhibit cooperation in the telecommunications and superconductor sectors.

- Cooperation in the industrial sector is constrained by the need for confidentiality of agreements, interest in protection of intellectual property, difficulties in the transfer of funds, complex contracts and licensing procedures, and inefficient communications.[7]

A list of problems encountered by American scientists at the working level is also instructive:

- The cultural and economic differences between Russia and the United States present a significant chasm that must be bridged.

- For the next several years, the young Russians will emigrate to the West at every opportunity.

- Funds from the United States are sometimes skimmed by gangsters.

- Due to shortages of chemicals and supplies, it is usually impractical to conduct research in Moscow.

- Russian reluctance to undertake joint research is due to the pitiful state of their instrumentation.

- Russian personnel seem extremely competent, but their facilities are antiquated and substandard.

- One particular institute has rented its best space on the bottom floor to a car dealership to pay for power and heating.

- While the publication record of most Russian research groups is excellent, the material is lost in Russian-language articles that Americans never see.

- In every institute there are a few scientists who are definitely among the top in the world, but most of their work remains unknown outside Russia.

- The average level of Russian science is rather low. Most scientists are not as knowledgeable, hard-working, or enthusiastic about research as their Western counterparts.

- Many Russian scientists who used to be at the top of the pecking order are very defensive and feel that they have lost all.[8]

The conclusions of most reports of American participants in joint programs emphasize that the experience was professionally and personally rewarding. Somehow, American scientists are always able to sift technical nuggets and to discern glimmers of optimism from their Russian colleagues, who have often been deprived of even the most basic support systems on the job.

LESSONS LEARNED

A great deal has been discovered, usually by trial and error, about the ingredients necessary for success in carrying out cooperative programs. Discussions with hundreds of U.S. and Russian government officials, practitioners, and organizations investing their time, energy, and financial resources in cooperative ventures have contributed to the formulation of a short list of lessons learned, presented here.

1. *Recognize that Russia Is Different.* While shock therapy may have been successful in Poland and privatization may have transformed the Czech Republic, recent history vividly underscores the differences in trying to foster change in Russia. Russia has unique problems, capabilities, and heritage—in politics, economics, and science. The models for the country to follow should be "made in Russia," whether they relate to privatization of industry, energy strategies, environmental cleanup, or the organization and funding of research. Use the Russian experience, and not the American experience in other countries, as the point of departure in designing cooperative programs.

2. *Move Away from Regional Approaches Involving All the Former Soviet States.* While administratively convenient, U.S. programs of cooperation designed to embrace not only Russia but the other former Soviet states present many distortions in their treatment of Russia. Recognizing this reality is particularly important in science and technology, given Moscow's overwhelming advantages in technical manpower and related resources. Clearly, U.S. agencies in science and technology should focus on designing programs exclusively for Russia, while separate programs address the other successor states and their special needs.

3. *Appreciate the Importance of Foreign Cooperation.* Few significant research projects are under way in Russia that do not involve Western participants. This almost always means that the foreigners are paying a disproportionate share of the costs. Without such participation, a large portion of the Russian research establishment would slide into dormancy. If Washington considers a Russian project to be truly important, American specialists should be encouraged—financially or otherwise—to become involved in it.[9]

4. *Replace Technical Assistance with Technical Cooperation.* Technical assistance is a donor-recipient concept, often likened to a doctor-patient relationship, that was imported into Russia from the third world. It is not an appropriate basis—politically or technically—for effective programs, particularly in science and technology. The term, the concept, and the associated activities should be put aside in favor of *technical cooperation,* which entails joint participation in development of original research concepts, distribution of funding responsibilities, and equitable sharing of the results of joint endeavors.[10]

5. *Give Priority to the Details of Implementation.* The details of program implementation are critically important to success in Russia. Many aspects of projects cannot be anticipated until these are well in progress, and the skill with which such operational technicalities are handled is no less important than the skill in developing and negotiating the overall approach. It makes no sense for a professor to develop a cooperative program in Russia and then turn it over to a graduate assistant for implementation.

6. *Seek Russian Government Approvals—Gingerly.* Obtaining formal governmental approvals in Moscow for cooperative projects is not a trivial undertaking. For short-term programs involving modest sums of money, official sanctions are usually not worth the effort. But for lengthier ones, such approvals are very valuable, even if they delay implementation for many months. Sooner or later the tax inspectors, the customs officials, and the trade unions will take an interest in the programs, and formal documentation eases the problems in dealing with these and other agents in search of foreign dollars.

7. *Put It in Writing.* The opportunities for misunderstandings over the details of cooperative activities are legendary. While trust between American and Russian colleagues has increased dramatically in recent years, the handshake has not yet become the vehicle for agreeing on collaborative activities. Of special importance is a clear understanding of the financial obligations of each party. Preparing a document that sets forth such obligations provides the added benefit of forcing all concerned to think through all the financial details at a time when even tickets for the metro are significant budgetary items. But once agreement has been reached in writing, do not expect flexibility on the Russian side. Documents are usually taken very seriously by Russians and followed to the letter.

8. *Recognize that Information Has a Price.* Technical data and related information, other than advertising brochures, provided free of charge by Russian organizations should be viewed with suspicion. If the information is useful to technical specialists, it usually has a price tag.

9. *Train the Real Russian Managers.* Management training has been one of the most popular programs supported by assistance agencies and has also become the topic *du jour* within many Russian educational institutions. However, most overseas training offered to Russian managers has been wasted. Management training will have near-term impact only when it is tailored to the specific responsibilities that the trainees will encounter at the conclusion of the course. General management training to prepare Russian professionals for employment in mythical positions back home is seldom cost-effective.[11]

10. *Train the American Managers.* Few American managers have an appreciation of Russian accounting procedures, the Russian concept of profit, or Russian labor laws. Too often these self-styled American reformers fail to make an impact simply because they did not take the time to consider how Russian management practices and American approaches can be most usefully combined. Also, American managers would be well advised to have some immersion in Russian history and culture before arriving at Sheremetyevo Airport.

11. *Pay by the Day.* Given the declining work ethic in the country— which may mean annual vacations of two months, frequent sick days, and additional time off for social obligations—foreigners should be wary of providing annual or even monthly salaries for Russian participants in projects. Rather, payment calculated on a daily basis for actual days worked avoids the absentee syndrome. It is advisable to pay by the day but pay generously in order to provide a cushion for reasonable employee benefits.[12]

12. *Forget "Emergency" Aid for Scientists.* Since the economic crisis among Russian researchers will last indefinitely, the concept of emergency aid from abroad to "tide them over" with salary supplements for six months to one year has never made much sense. Indeed, some recipients of small "emergency" grants provided several years ago by American organizations are no longer in their laboratories. Only in a limited number of cases was the aid pivotal in keeping researchers at the bench for more than a few months.

13. *Don't Ignore the Research Infrastructure.* Even generous grants to Russian scientists may be inadequate to ensure high-quality research. One must pay for the upkeep of the working space as well, and Russian institutions increasingly have no money for electricity or telephones, let alone spare parts and materials. Overhead payments of 10–20 percent included in some small grants from abroad are important symbolically but have little impact on the problem. Only the Russian government itself, possibly supported by the World Bank, is capable of financing the widely needed laboratory upgrades. Until such action is taken, project coordinators should anticipate disruptions springing from breakdowns in the research infrastructure.

14. *Question the Realism of Russian Research Proposals.* American reviewers of Russian research proposals, in a sincere effort to help their foreign colleagues, often rank such proposals higher in terms of scientific merit than they would rank those of American researchers—particularly if the Russians are not in competition with Americans for the same pool of funds. In addition, the American reviewers may not be aware of the extent of the decline in laboratory conditions in Russia. Therefore, American funding organizations should adopt a clear-eyed view of the constraints on free-ranging scientific inquiry so as not to be disappointed with Russian results obtained under most difficult conditions.

15. *Rely on Russian Ability to Develop Proposals.* If given detailed guidelines and reasonable financial incentives, Russian specialists can develop well-framed proposals that are more appropriate to the Russian setting than those that could be developed by American consultants or scientists. Of course, as just mentioned, the Russians may promise more than they can deliver. Nevertheless, the cooperative programs that have recognized and relied on native capabilities rather than on American experts in shaping the Russian contribution have usually been the most successful.[13]

16. *Recognize the Long-standing History of Russian Peer Review.* Americans did not introduce Russian scientists to peer review. The Soviet Union had more variations of peer review of project proposals, scientific articles submitted for publication, and candidates for scientific awards than can be imagined. The primary problems were the biased selection of reviewers by managers tied into the party networks and the closed nature of the process that excluded many potentially interested researchers from competing for funds. In their interactions with Russian counterparts, U.S. organizations should focus on countering the harmful legacy of these practices rather than dictating whether panels of peers, individual reviewers, or other organizational variations of the peer-review process will work best.

17. *Accept the Reality of the Internal Brain Drain.* Relatively few active researchers, numbering in the thousands, have emigrated from Russia since 1992, but many tens of thousands,

particularly young researchers, have left laboratories for more profitable endeavors in the banks, the commercial offices, and even the kiosks of Russia. Sponsorships are seldom available to replace the departees with other young candidates. Innovative cooperative programs are needed to help prevent the complete loss of an entire generation of Russian researchers.[14]

18. *Find Interested Audiences before Launching Demonstration Projects.* Replication, presumably, is the objective of cooperative demonstration projects. However, unless there is someone well connected standing in the wings with adequate financial support to build on the success of the demonstration project, its purpose becomes very uncertain. Those with the potential to carry through replication should be identified prior to initiation of a demonstration project and invited to participate from the outset.

19. *Support Both Large and Small Projects.* In general, large cooperative projects involving sizable Russian research teams will have a more lasting impact than clusters of small projects. Usually, the larger the project, the greater the official Russian interest, and the greater the likelihood of Moscow's commitment to follow-on activities. But it is also true that some of the most creative scientists and engineers work as individuals or as leaders of very small teams. The costs to support them on an annual basis as they develop their ideas may be much smaller than the costs of supporting large teams of specialists of mixed capabilities. However, they must be sustained on a steady basis for a number of years to be fully effective. In addition, the administrative problems of establishing a single, small cooperative project may be as great as those associated with a much larger one.

20. *Automate the Russian Way.* Western computers are often underutilized in Russia if adequate funds are not available for the recipient to ensure that the appropriate software is properly installed, that there is protection against power surges, and that paper is available for the printers. Often modems lie idle because of an absence of telephone lines. The idea of computer networks is conceptually sound, but the cost of hiring a systems manager is often prohibitive. E-mail is the modern way, but fax is still the Russian way—in most institutions.

21. *Anticipate the Ubiquitous Tax Inspector.* Western sources of funds have attracted and retained the interest of tax inspectors throughout the country who will continue to search for their expected cuts. Tax exemptions are the prerogative of the Duma, but enforcement is the responsibility of the tax inspector. The likelihood of parliamentary tax relief is less meaningful when the benevolence of the functionary responsible for collecting revenue cannot be counted upon.

22. *Do Not Assume that Funds Transferred to Institutes Will Reach Researchers Intact.* With few exceptions, only a small percentage of funds transferred to Russian institutes for joint projects reaches the researchers (generally about 15 percent). The deductions for overhead, taxes, social funds, and government payments are simply very large.[15] The most effective way to avoid such subtractions is to concentrate financial support on providing equipment and on covering the costs of travel and per diem expenses for trips to the United States by direct payments to the travelers. Should the transfer of funds to individual Russian scientists be an important aspect of a project, then the ISTC and CRDF approaches of transferring funds to individuals rather than institute bank accounts should be carefully reviewed as possible models for replication.

23. *Resolve Disputes over Vodka, Not in the Courts.* The most serious disputes between Russian and American partners almost always involve money. While lawyers may suggest going to court in Russia if the stakes are large enough, aggrieved Americans should remember that a favorable court decision is not synonymous with collecting bad debts. The Russian way with a problem is to discuss, discuss, and discuss again; more often than one would imagine, a settlement is eventually reached.[16]

Certainly, a great deal has been learned by Americans collectively about carrying out effective programs with Russian colleagues. America's investment practices during a period of trial and error have mounted a steep learning curve; with that experience behind, more time can now be devoted to productive interaction. In short, many American organizations are poised to realize more bang for the buck.[17]

THE OUTLOOK FOR COOPERATION

Beyond a learning experience in the pitfalls of doing business in Russia, what has been the return to the United States on its investment of almost $5 billion (equivalent to the cost of one aircraft carrier and operating it for a year) in redirecting Russian know-how?[18] Against this background, what is the future for bilateral cooperation in science and technology?

Visits to the Proton rocket line at the Khrunichev Space Production Organization in Moscow, to the pulsed power facility at the Institute of Experimental Physics in Arzamas-16, or to the biological hot cells at the Vector Center for Virology and Biotechnology in Koltsovo will impress even the most conservative senator as to how American cooperative efforts have penetrated the very heart of the military-industrial complex of the former Soviet Union. Just a few years ago, the United States would have paid an inordinate sum simply to have such access, let alone share in some of the latest technological secrets of its erstwhile rival. In addition, the payoff from bilateral projects that help contain within Russia some of the most destructive technologies ever developed is beyond measurement. Clearly, in the area of national security, the United States has received handsome returns on its investment.

As for individual American firms, each daily Delta Airlines flight from New York to Moscow is crowded with American entrepreneurs searching for new opportunities to cash in on the Russian reservoirs of technological achievement and natural resources. If the enthusiasm of these transatlantic travelers on their flights back to New York is any measure, the return to them on investments of both the U.S. government and the private sector itself is sufficient and growing.

Meanwhile, other programs have yielded benefits for society as a whole. NASA contends that its joint program with Russia is saving the American taxpayer at least $2 billion, the would-be cost for replicating Soviet technologies in the United States.[19] Measures in ecological and public health management to limit pollution problems, destructive pests, and human diseases at their sources prevent massive costs of remedial actions in the United States. In the long run, Russian commitments to energy conservation and sustainable development inspired during transatlantic exchanges will help maintain the stability of the biosphere.

Yes, despite the many imperfections in bilateral programs, the American people have had their investment in Russian know-how repaid many times over. Moreover, the United States now has in place an unparalleled network of organizational and administrative arrangements for cooperation manned by a large cadre of specialists who have learned the ropes for working in Russia. Given that there is unfinished business in Russia—the opportunities for still greater returns on prior investments as well as on new ones—it would make no sense to abandon the broad-based program of interactions currently under way.

In short, the case for large-scale cooperation in science and technology has been repeatedly made on the ground in Russia. The gains that serve America's interests in national security, foreign trade, environmental protection, space exploration, and scientific discovery are impressive— exceeding the boldest imaginations of even the optimists of the late 1980s.

While technical assistance strictly speaking may be an obsolete concept for all concerned, genuine cooperation in many areas of science and technology based on mutual anticipated benefits can and should be a cornerstone of the Russian-American relationship in the years ahead. In Russia, the outlook for cooperation in science and technology remains bright, despite the continued opposition of vocal reactionaries scattered throughout the country. At all levels, Russian officials and specialists continue to acknowledge and admire the technological achievements of the United States. In Washington, however, finding funds to support cooperation in any field will become increasingly difficult. Of special concern in the near term is the critical importance of directing funds appropriated pursuant to the Freedom Support Act to the strengthening of some strands of the science and technology relationship. In a fair competition among advocates of programs focused on different sectors, the science and technology proponents can surely make one of the most convincing cases.

CHAPTER 6

FUTURE DIRECTIONS IN
SCIENCE AND TECHNOLOGY COOPERATION

The U.S. assistance effort is intended to be a temporary effort, and it is designed to facilitate the establishment of normal relations emphasizing cooperation.

Special Adviser to the U.S. President on Assistance
to the Newly Independent States
April 1996

If it doesn't sell, I don't want to invent it.

Thomas Edison
Early 1900s

BILATERAL COOPERATION AND POLITICAL OBJECTIVES

OLD AND NEW EXPECTATIONS

It is now clear that the Freedom Support Act and the Soviet Nuclear Threat Reduction Act (Nunn-Lugar) raised unrealistic expectations both in the United States and Russia over the ease of the transformation of Russia into a democratic, market-oriented, and nuclear-secure nation. The cooperative programs initiated under these legislative headings and through other bilateral channels, however, have played an important role in encouraging Russian leaders and institutions to develop and implement many policies and programs consistent with American views as to an appropriate course for that country.[1]

Science and technology has not been singled out in the U.S. budget process as a high-priority area for assistance to the former Soviet Union, yet cooperation in a variety of technical fields has flourished under both major legislative mandates. Scientists and engineers clearly must play a central role in projects related to reducing the dangers from weapons of mass destruction, and technical specialists will continue to be omnipresent in the Cooperative Threat Reduction (CTR) program. With regard to the Freedom Support Act, the U.S. Agency for International Development (AID) quickly recognized that U.S. technical agencies had considerable experience and interests in Russia and that it should not limit its efforts to supporting only those political and economic figures who had immediate responsibility for weaving the new reform fabric of Russia. With many scientists and engineers placed in critical positions within the Russian government, it was not surprising that AID soon involved the technical communities in both countries in its programs. Projects in health, energy, environment, defense conversion, and other technical fields were justified as essential in easing the burdens on the population during the political and economic transition.

During the congressional appropriations processes, many U.S. technical agencies were also able to ride the crest of interest in Washington in capitalizing on Russian capabilities while at the same time influencing developments in the country. Perhaps the best examples are the roles of NASA and the Department of Energy, which have created dense webs of bilateral interactions among specialists in militarily sensitive fields— interactions that have contributed dramatically to enhancing American national security interests. Many technical experts from throughout the U.S. government now seem to have commuter passes to Moscow.

The American private sector followed the government's lead; soon the presence in Russia of organizations from across the United States, including many high-technology companies and several corporate and private foundations with interests in ecology and basic science, was far more extensive than anyone would have imagined just a few years before. If the development within Russia of many independent centers for mobilizing the energies of the population is a goal of peace advocates, American scientists and engineers can be said to have contributed their share to the evolution of a civil society with peaceful aspirations.

DIFFERENT INTERPRETATIONS OF HISTORY

Whether American programs have made a major difference in changing for the better the political, economic, and technical landscape of Russia will be debated for years. With regard to foreign economic assistance, some American historians will probably report that AID programs provided critical reinforcement for the efforts of many progressives in shaping an emerging civil society—including scientists who regularly criticized the same autocratic approaches of Russian officials they had earlier challenged under the Soviet regime. Others may conclude that AID programs were temporary crutches that simply supported false hopes within the enterprises and institutes. Russian enthusiasts will undoubtedly point to the golden days of foreign aid that helped them bridge the gaps between erratic paychecks and reduced temptations to join the brain drain. Some Russian critics will surely relive current frustrations, claiming that Russia moved toward becoming a nation of beggars, with its professors transformed into paupers, as the United States misled the country with visions of instant prosperity.

In the national security arena, the judgments will probably also be contradictory. *Defense by other means*, the essence of the CTR program, is still hailed as a valid concept by many influential politicians in both countries who weigh the evidence of progress made during the past several years. Photographs of destroyed missiles and submarines in Russia, samples of hearing aids and solar panels made in former defense enterprises, and reports of nuclear warheads rendered inoperative are impressive. But the long delays in constructing facilities for storing nuclear weapons materials and for destroying chemical weapons continue to nag at the implementers. Also, questions will linger as to how much of the money designated for decommissioning and conversion projects in Russia really found its way to its destination.

The linkage between CTR activities and foreign economic assistance has been difficult to uncouple. This association has provided a convenient target for those congressional skeptics who are inclined to attack all programs in Russia as giveaways. Some frequently urge increased defense expenditures in their own home districts rather than reductions in a nuclear or missile threat that emanates from Russia.

Perhaps surprisingly, Russian interest in cooperative endeavors in national security areas seems to be holding steady despite retrenchments forced by the conservatives. Russian leaders have become accustomed to discussing sensitive issues openly, to seeing foreigners wander the halls of previously secret facilities, and to unlocking their financial records for American auditors. Further, shifts in American policies now permit the hiring of Russian subcontractors for American-financed construction projects in Russia, and the United States is willing to accept Russian suggestions for modifications in technical approaches. These developments renewed Russian enthusiasm. And, as previously noted, there has been a sharp increase in regular interactions between the Russian and American nuclear and space communities—from the most senior officials to the bench scientists—to contend with major security issues.[2]

Scientists and engineers have participated in bilateral exchanges in recent years with an intensity that will not again be matched. As their mutual engagement declines, they must pay greater attention to ways in which more limited involvement can be as effective as the broader participation of the past.

Benefits as the Criteria of Success

The arguments for devoting substantial U.S. government financial resources to science and technology programs in Russia remain persuasive. Many difficulties facing Russia have global implications—energy production shortfalls, releases of environmental pollutants, health problems, nuclear accidents. Russia's underdeveloped storehouse of natural resources, immature consumer markets, and highly skilled manpower pool also continue to entice American commercial and scientific organizations.

From the Russian side, a principal reason for cooperation with the United States continues to be the need for as many overseas sources of financing as possible. However, this rationale is not as strong as in the past, given Russian perceptions of failures on the American side to deliver aid at anticipated levels and growing convictions in political circles that erosion of national sovereignty is too high a price for receiving support from abroad. Russian scientists are increasingly adept at finding new routes to financial survival (albeit often along paths more commercial than scholarly), but few have found a substitute for international linkages when it comes to advancing their professional careers.

Whenever U.S. government funding or endorsement for a science or technology proposal is required, the first questions of American budgeteers will more frequently relate to the specific, near-term benefits accruing to the United States from the particular program. Generalized benefits have been articulated for years. But general rhetoric about project successes is easy to ignore; meaningful, tangible results associated with concrete projects are not.

With regard to cooperative projects at Russian nuclear weapons institutes, to take one example, a checklist for assessing outcomes of interest to the United States might include:

- Did the project strengthen local capabilities to prevent the theft of nuclear materials stored at the institute hosting the project?

- Did the project reduce the temptation for institute researchers to look for opportunities in rogue states?

- Did the project result in permanent redirection of the energies of weapons personnel or conversion of facilities to civilian activities?

- Did the project increase the transparency of activities within a previously closed institute?

- Did the project generate information that might interest American scientific or commercial organizations?

- Did the project attract the interest of regional authorities who could use the institute's capabilities to increase economic stability in their region?

- Did the project introduce Western management and accounting techniques that could foster market-oriented approaches, even at the research stage?

Of no less importance than the checklist itself is the choice of the persons selected to answer these questions. The issues that have been raised above go to the heart of the developing economic, security, and research infrastructures in the country; and therefore analysis will be a challenge even for the most sophisticated foreign observer. Yet attempts should be made by specialists who are well trained in science and in management, who are highly experienced in Russian affairs, and who are sensitive to the importance of finding objective measures of success.

In Washington, the time of elusive expectations has expired. A new era consumed by results has begun. In Moscow—and in Magadan and Pushchino—the process of attracting financial and professional support from abroad continues, with no end in view.

STAYING THE COURSE WITH SUCCESS STORIES

ENCOURAGEMENT FROM THE GORE-CHERNOMYRDIN COMMISSION

The regular meetings between the American vice president and the Russian prime minister have provided important impetus to programs that were mired in the mud of sluggish bureaucracies. Despite the aspirations of American scientists and industrialists to have uninhibited communications and interactions with their Russian colleagues in all areas of endeavor, Russia is still Russia. Russian officials will likely play a central role not only in the budgetary and tax processes but in many other aspects of cooperation as well. And on the U.S. side, budget monitors will not easily entrust to the discretion of scientists the expenditures of large sums of money in the institutions of a country plagued by too many incidents of uncertain fiscal accountability. Thus, occasional pressure from the top can assist program managers in moving their activities through the bureaucratic morasses in both countries.

Beyond lowering the administrative barriers to project implementation, the Gore-Chernomyrdin Commission can continue to figure importantly in U.S.-Russian relations in additional ways. The fact that the regularly scheduled meetings are held sends important signals to the rest of the world that bilateral relations are on a positive course. Focusing attention on specific areas of cooperation helps sets priorities within both governments. And the off-line discussions of outstanding political issues, from a nuclear test ban to international responses to turmoil in other successor states of the former Soviet Union, often clarify problems that may have become confused through normal diplomatic channels.

For more than three years, the commission has concentrated on immediate opportunities to move specific projects forward. Now, a look at U.S.-Russian cooperation from a larger perspective by the commission could be timely. Of special interest are steps to fill the void as U.S. foreign economic assistance is scaled back drastically. A special, bilateral group of public- and private-sector representatives, acting under the auspices of the commission, should be able to develop practical suggestions for building on past successes in collaboration.

One critical question is whether the commission has become too personalized. The mutual interests in cooperation and the track record of the commission suggest, however, that should the vice president or the prime minister depart from the political scene, the two governments will find an alternative approach to maintain a dialogue that helps clear the obstacles to project agreement and implementation.

Efforts of the commission's eight committees and their staffs, as well as those of several White House offices, the Department of State, and others, to coordinate U.S. activities in Russia have been enormous. However, one important issue has been neglected and now needs serious attention; namely, confusion in Washington as to what is assistance and what is not assistance, and the attendant need to articulate the differences carefully and repeatedly. The confusion is reflected in documents developed by those responsible for coordination, in their congressional testimony, and in public statements made by an array of changing staff members.

EXPANDING THE NUNN-LUGAR MANDATE

The likelihood of nuclear proliferation from Russian origins has been reduced thanks to the CTR program. But despite significant progress, there is still a long way to go in reducing such a possibility to an acceptable minimum. Also, the threats of proliferation of missile technology and of the components and know-how for biological and chemical weapons remain very large. While not the only source of dangerous technologies with ominous implications for the world, Russia is near the top of the list.

From the very beginning, the image of the Nunn-Lugar legislation as a foreign aid program has not played well in Moscow or Washington. Also, continuation of the program has become entangled in several inflammatory issues such as sales of highly enriched uranium by Russia to the United States, Russian offers of nuclear reactor components to Iran, and questions concerning Russian compliance with obligations to stop certain research activities related to biological weapons. Nevertheless, program implementation is generally on track; joint efforts are proceeding on a number of fronts.

An amended version of the legislation—often referred to as Nunn-Lugar-Domenici—has been passed by Congress. This legislation also includes measures to counter the threats of terrorism in the United States, and it gained the unprecedented support of all members of the Senate. This surely reflects satisfaction with the original Nunn-Lugar legislation, in spite of the problems noted above. Still, the same types of political obstacles will again arise in the debates over appropriations.

The program should be recast as a global effort rather than as a program exclusively for the former Soviet Union. The United States is in a good position to move immediately in that direction. For instance, improving the protection of sensitive nuclear materials in a number of countries is of growing concern. A global approach would probably be more palatable in Russia; indeed, the Russians have much to offer outside their own borders. Also, the global approach would help remove the program from the controversial Russian aid debate. Does this mean that the program would begin to operate in China, India, North Korea, and elsewhere? Yes—on a modest scale, at appropriate times, and in different ways.

To help ensure that the Nunn-Lugar concepts and the CTR program method do not fade away with political changes in Washington, more detailed assessments than are possible in this book compiled by well-established institutions could help to commit to collective memory and to perpetuate past policy initiatives that have proved successful. Meanwhile, a major public education drive is needed in the United States and in Russia to broaden appreciation of the objectives and achievements of many of the specific projects.[3]

FURTHER RELIANCE ON RUSSIAN SPACE TECHNOLOGY

The importance to NASA of relying on Russian technical capabilities was not fully appreciated outside that organization during the early 1990s, but within a few years of the Soviet Union's breakup NASA's program became the largest single component of science and technology cooperation between the two countries. The cost savings to the United States in capitalizing on Soviet investments are substantial. These joint explorations should continue to be a sound financial investment for the United States, provided Russian technical performance continues at a high level, with significant side benefits in advancing U.S. political and security interests.

That is not to say, however, that other political or financial issues will never threaten the program. But the American and Russian human space flight programs have been integrated to such an extent that even if the most conservative political parties become dominant within Russia, that country will have great difficulty withdrawing. Russia simply will not have the resources to retrofit its program and move forward on its own at a pace that would enable it to remain among the leaders in the exploration of space.

ENCOURAGING PRIVATE-SECTOR ACTIVITIES

Congressional support for public financing of incentive programs related to trade and investment seems solid despite recent attempts to abolish the Overseas Private Investment Corporation in its entirety. On Capitol Hill, "private sector" is the mantra chanted in hopes of propelling Russia in the right direction. And what better mechanism could there be, argue both conservatives and liberals, than deeper involvement of the American private sector in modernization of the country? The constraints are largely a function of the unfriendly business environment in Russia, but Washington will presumably continue its efforts to reduce financial uncertainties and to ease the problems of doing business in the country.

In Moscow, however, considerable suspicion lingers over the intentions of foreign firms, notwithstanding repeated calls by the government for increased foreign investment. Industrial espionage, unfair distribution of intellectual property rights, and schemes to evade tax collection are perennial criticisms of the behavior of Western companies. While specific American companies are seldom singled out for such attacks, general pronouncements cannot go unnoticed in Washington since the most numerous among the foreign firms operating in Russia are the Americans.

Overall, the outlook for the U.S. private sector in Russia is positive. The U.S. government can assist in clearing away many of the briar patches along the road, and private firms seem prepared to retain a strong presence in the country.

NEW PROGRAM INITIATIVES

FILLING THE VOID AS AID DEPARTS

U.S. economic assistance allocated to Russia may soon dip to $50 to 100 million per year or lower, a sharp contrast to the figure for 1994, which exceeded $1 billion.[4] These cutbacks will be felt by many U.S. government agencies, private contractors, and nongovernmental organizations that have developed a deep dependence on AID funding.

If given the chance to present proposals that receive objective consideration by the U.S. government, science and technology advocates should be able to compete successfully for the dwindling funds, even if projects must be justified on the basis of their near-term contributions to political reform. With its traditions of factual objectivity, independence of thought, openness to self-criticism, and individual initiative, the American scientific community offers a model that has broad relevance to the type of society that Western nations hope will emerge in Russia.

As AID terminates its programs, many important institutions in Russia will have their financial umbilical cords to American partners severed, with the possibility that the fruits of past AID investments may quickly disappear. AID should consider practical steps to help cushion the impact. For example, existing funds could be effectively redeployed to advance money to well-established and successful programs for phase-out periods of three years.

Of particular concern are the budgets of U.S. government agencies that were folded into the Freedom Support Act portfolio in 1992 in view of the congressional desire for increased coordination. One significant case is the program of the United States Information Agency. Few will deny the benefits to the United States of exchange programs that bring across the ocean carefully selected Russian leaders and students, including many with a penchant for science; it is desirable that such activities continue.

Ambitious alternatives to AID programs have been developed by nongovernmental organizations in the United States, including establishment of new agencies to administer economic development funds appropriated by Congress for Russia. Such sweeping proposals to transform AID, or some of its responsibilities, are simply beyond the scope of this book. They should be considered within the broader context of the reorganization of U.S. foreign assistance programs on a worldwide basis.[5]

A FUND FOR BILATERAL COOPERATION BETWEEN TECHNICAL AGENCIES

With AID likely to reduce its presence in Russia, an important source of funds for a number of government agencies with well-developed linkages to counterpart organizations in Russia may disappear. These agencies primarily need travel funds to support exchange visits by their specialists and, when appropriate, by Russian counterparts. A centrally managed program of a few million dollars annually would cover the costs of airline tickets and travel expenses and thereby allow the two dozen agencies concerned to build on the trust and mutual interests that have developed between Russia and the United States during the early 1990s. This issue needs prompt attention by both the executive branch and Congress.

THE CIVILIAN RESEARCH AND DEVELOPMENT FOUNDATION

As discussed in an earlier chapter, after three years of effort, in late 1995 the National Science Foundation established the Civilian Research and Development Foundation (CRDF).[6] With an initial budget of $10 million, the new foundation solicited proposals from many Russian researchers. The initial experience clearly demonstrated that there are many good Russian proposals for collaborative research that await financial support. The CRDF should become the Clinton administration's principal mechanism for supporting Russian researchers in institutions that were not intimately tied to the Soviet military effort. But this will only happen with a major infusion of funds.

The concept of the foundation was triggered by the favorable experience of three binational foundations in Israel that were financed partially by

American assets with a value exceeding $400 million (in current U.S. dollars). These foundations support research and development activities that have handsomely benefited both Israel and the United States.[7]

The United States should be prepared to contribute at least $100 million, for allocation over a ten-year period, to CRDF activities in Russia. While Russia's research potential has slipped significantly in recent years, many excellent researchers are still in place and are capable of contributing to laboratory investigations of international interest. In the past, as AID concluded its programs in some countries, Congress left behind "graduation presents" so that the United States could continue to capitalize on U.S. investments and on the countries' capabilities. What better AID departure gift could Congress offer than an endowment that will enable Russia, the United States, and the rest of the world to benefit from the hundreds of billions of dollars that the Soviet Union invested in science and technology and the hundreds of millions of dollars that the United States has more recently invested in Russian researchers?

Should these additional resources become available, the CRDF ought to change its emphasis from providing small grants (up to $40,000 per year for two years) to larger and longer awards. Eventually, the length of the award rather than its size should be the key consideration. The distribution of support among many recipients has been a popular approach in eliciting public support from Russian and American scientists. But spreading money so thinly is unlikely to have much impact on the state of Russian science. Larger and longer grants would ensure that at least a few research groups were able to survive, better yet thrive, with a corresponding payoff for international science. The approach of the Howard Hughes Medical Institute in providing five-year grants totaling up to $150,000 each seems relevant in this regard. A few lasting footprints in concrete are better than many in the sand that quickly disappear.

CONVERSION AND COMMERCIALIZATION IN THE DEFENSE SECTOR

Conventional wisdom in Washington is that Congress does not like defense conversion projects and that this label should be dropped from all U.S.-funded activities. This view is shortsighted. Congress should support destruction of the capabilities to produce military hardware with just as much vigor as it supports destruction of the hardware itself. If *irreversible* conversion of the production lines keeps weapons scientists and engineers occupied with civilian activities, so much the better.

The Russians say this is not how defense conversion works. They simply expect a defense enterprise to produce a civilian product, without regard to whether that means permanently closing a military production line. This is not conversion but *diversification*, which became a goal of the Soviet Union from the 1960s onward. Worthy in terms of economic development, diversification nevertheless cannot justify U.S. financial support that is awarded purely on the basis of national security considerations.

Past U.S. support of defense diversification in Russia has been channeled through American companies that enter into joint ventures or other business alliances with former Soviet defense enterprises. By providing financial backing for the initial activities of the American firms, the U.S. government encourages them to invest their own resources in establishing a long-term presence in Russia. This approach has resulted in very modest achievements in converting important military production lines to processes that produce civilian goods. The American firms clearly are only interested in producing salable products, not in worrying about the latent defense capacity of the Russian partner.

Now, despite this confusion between defense diversification and conversion, the two governments have agreed to consider seriously the issue of "technology commercialization."[8] The Russian defense plants figure most prominently in developing the idea. Given U.S. national security interests in the future of these plants, the discussion should be broader than simply stimulation of U.S. investment in Russia in commercial production. It should reach to the core of the concepts of conversion and diversification to determine if there are appropriate ways for the U.S. government to encourage true conversion.

One primary need of Russian enterprises is investment capital. Of course, management and marketing skills are important; but capital remains a key. If conversion is at stake, the U.S. government should be especially interested. Development banks in Russia that will support loans directly to Russian enterprises for technological innovation and initial production runs—with payback periods of up to five years—could make a difference in a country that has become captive to the whims of Western investors. Limited local efforts in this direction have been attempted but with little enthusiasm by the banks and less success by the entrepreneurs in obtaining capital. Now, the United States, acting through the international financial institutions, which have considerable experience in this area, could play an important role in encouraging capital infusions that can lead toward more meaningful conversion and commercialization.

ATTENDING TO PROGRAM "DETAILS"

TAXES, CUSTOMS, AND INTELLECTUAL PROPERTY RIGHTS

Progress is finally being made in removing some of the major administrative barriers to implementing bilateral science and technology agreements. The Duma has enacted a new law to grant "tax-free" status to funds transferred to local scientists from abroad to support their research activities. (See Appendix I.) It has also enacted legislation that should grant customs privileges for equipment being imported into Russia in cooperation with bilateral space research projects. (See Appendix J.) And the two governments have reached agreement on principles concerning intellectual property rights that should be considered by government agencies entering into bilateral arrangements. (See Appendix K.)

But these issues will remain prickly. The delay at the customs office at Sheremetyevo Airport may be shorter, but it will not disappear. The Russian and American government lawyers will have many more meetings on patent issues. The Russian tax collectors will not go away, as they interpret new regulations in ways that may be alien to American experts. The Department of State and the Ministry of Science and Technology Policy (recently renamed the State Committee for Science and Technology) should be given high marks for their struggles to resolve these knotty issues. But they need to continue to focus on them whenever possible.

PAYING SALARIES OF RUSSIAN PROJECT PARTICIPANTS

The cooperative spirit in science and technology has demonstrated an uncanny ability to survive even the most violent political upheavals in Russia. However, cooperation cannot surmount a total lack of financial support. When funds are available for a project, the advocates in both countries somehow find a way to carry out that project. Implementation may not always be pretty, but usually the positive results outweigh the negative.

In Soviet times, Russians equated the costs of cooperation with travel expenses, purchases of specialized equipment, and other direct outlays for a project, whereas the Americans usually included the salaries of their personnel and the overhead of the participating American institutions. While Russian institute directors are rapidly learning that they too should include personnel and overhead costs in their financing plans (particularly in the absence of such support from the Russian government), they often willingly participate simply for travel reimbursement.

Previously, when a delegation of ten specialists from the laboratories of the Department of Energy visited Russia for one week and the department put the cost at $100,000, Russian counterparts were confused because their abacus registered only $30,000 worth of travel expenses. After the Americans explained that the billing rate for specialists is between $1,200 and $1,500 per person per day, the Russians replied, "Just send us the money and not the advisers." Now Russian institutions understand that Americans must also be paid, but they have difficulty accepting the disparity in salaries that is involved.[9] The best tactic for U.S. organizations is simply not to discuss with Russian colleagues the salaries of Americans involved in cooperation since the topic only causes unnecessary friction.

Central to consideration of the costs of projects is the issue of whether U.S. Government funds should be used to pay the salaries of Russian participants in joint projects. How critical is the engagement of certain Russian scientists in a project, and how decisive is a salary supplement in maintaining their interest in it?

In the national security area, the United States should continue to pay salaries, at least for several more years. The stakes are simply too high not to do so. The programs should be kept as attractive as possible for Russian specialists from the heart of the weapons complex. Perhaps this is a form of nonproliferation bribery, but Western payoffs for peace are better than Middle Eastern baksheesh for armaments.

A similar approach seems desirable, though, for scientists who never served the Soviet military effort. If an overriding goal is to encourage the weaponeers to join the civilian community, then that community must be perceived as a place where rewards exist. It would be, in addition, unfair to discriminate against the civilian scientists simply because they had always followed less controversial pursuits.

That said, Western governments should phase out by the end of the decade their practice of subsidizing salaries for Russians. As the Russian economy slowly recovers, the Russian government must assume this most basic responsibility in ensuring a decent standard of living for its citizens. The longer that foreign funds are the source of salaries, the slower will be the transition to a responsible approach for managing the country's research and development. In time, American funds expended in Russia should be limited to providing equipment and supplies that support research of direct interest to the United States and to paying travel costs that facilitate interactions with American colleagues; these items will probably be considered by Moscow as "luxury" items for many years to come. As the millennium approaches, American institutions such as

NASA, CRDF, and the Department of Energy should disengage themselves from providing salaries to research groups throughout the country.

Enthusiastic participation of key Russian specialists is one of the most important elements in the success of any cooperative program. The salary question is so fundamental to their interests that it must be handled with the greatest care and not treated simply as another routine issue on the negotiating table.

PREPARING FOR THE END GAME

NASA, CRDF, and the Department of Energy are among the many American organizations funding two- and three-year projects at Russian research institutions. All of these organizations argue that they are helping to tide over the best Russian scientists until other funding sources emerge. But what are these other funding sources? In only a very few cases will Russian institutions come to the rescue with the scarce financial reserves that are available to them. The American agencies and other organizations, individually, and the U.S. government, as a whole, need to plan an end game for when their projects are completed. In some cases, U.S. industry may become interested, but such interest will be limited in many areas.

The Russian partners should not simply be dropped. The United States has much more to gain from many of the investments already made. As noted, Russian scientists often value their professional standing in the eyes of their American partners as much as they value the steady paychecks resulting from cooperation. Of course, they would like both. Nevertheless, given budget realities, they cannot have both indefinitely.

One end-game plan could ensure that when a successful bilateral project with untapped potential comes to the limit of its tenure, the U.S. funding agency will continue to support the relationship, perhaps at a much reduced level. In the parlance of exchange experts, the cooperating scientists would be "twinned" for a period of, say, three to five years, with the United States providing simply airplane tickets and per diem expenses for annual exchange visits by the collaborators.

THE BOTTOM LINE: MONEY

The bottom line in considering the future of cooperation is money—how much and how it is used. In the near term, the U.S. government has the key to the bank vault. The American science and technology communities must convince officials that they and their Russian partners have projects with sizable returns that warrant opening many drawers for disbursement in their names.

If the goal of the current U.S. assistance strategy is to facilitate movement toward a more "normal" bilateral relationship, what area is more appropriate for emphasis than science and technology? For decades, cooperation in broad areas of science and technology has buttressed U.S. relations with dozens of other countries throughout the world, and most of them have far weaker technical capabilities than Russia. Public investment now in order to establish a firm basis for sustained collaboration could go a long way in meeting the stated objective.

As the Russian government gradually adopts the philosophy of Thomas Edison—to emphasize research that has a marketable result—the United States and the world should increasingly benefit from a relighting of darkened Russian laboratories. Clearly, the best way to ensure that the revitalized lamps of learning illuminate the paths to peace rather than the well-worn ruts toward war is for American specialists to be involved in the transformation.

EPILOGUE

The West listens primarily to those Russian politicians who manipulate the vocabulary of Western liberal values, but who will play no vital role in Russia's future.

A leading Russian scholar
December 1995

Backing the wrong horse shouldn't matter if the pony that wins can be relied upon to have a decent relationship with the United States.

Newsweek
June 1996

PRAGMATISM AND COOPERATION

Meeting payrolls is still the primary concern of many Russian enterprise and institute directors. They have learned that the best sources of reliable funding have come from the West, and the largest sources have been in Washington. However, the scene is changing. The U.S. government is retrenching. No longer are programs justified on the basis of unprecedented access to previously closed institutions or opportunities to engage highly talented specialists in exploratory programs with potentially significant payoff. Now, *the value of the deliverables* has become the watchword when U.S. agencies enter into bilateral arrangements.

The American private sector has also become more pragmatic when initiating business deals in Russia, with a much sharper eye on the bottom line than in years past. The technological capabilities of Russian institutions still intrigue American companies, but these companies too need assurances that they will be able to use in a practical way the

123

products that emerge from the Russian laboratories where they invest their resources.

American sources available to finance work at Russian institutes will remain in place, but they will not be as deep nor as accessible as in the past. Meanwhile, more European and Asian organizations, which have lagged behind the Americans in discovering the technological strengths of Russia, are gradually emerging on the scene. Consequently, entrepreneurial Russian directors will increasingly head for Athens, Copenhagen, Seoul, Beijing, Taipei, and other neglected centers of financial resources—even to less well endowed cities in the developing world such as New Delhi and Saigon—in their searches for support.

As the wellsprings of offshore financing become more difficult to uncover, however, the aging directors of many institutes will undoubtedly think seriously about retirement. They may be content to look for funding within their ministries until their farewell parties. Dealing with foreign organizations may simply have become too complicated at this late stage in their careers.

Optimistic economists in Moscow and Washington predict that inflation has finally been capped, that the decline in industrial production has bottomed out, and that capital flight abroad will decline. Therefore, they contend, the economy is on the way to recovery. But, even if true, does this mean that the governmental budgets for research will also recover? With an underpaid and underhoused military establishment, coal miners on the verge of anarchy, and water and power systems that are on the brink of collapse, a major restoration of funds for scientific research seems somewhat unlikely. While the Duma may demand such increases, the Ministry of Finance will be unimpressed. So the outward reach for financial backing will continue, and indeed will probably intensify.

RESURGENCE OF THE RED-BROWNS AND
THE EFFECT ON COOPERATION

Whirling around the enterprise and institute directors is a political scene that has changed dramatically since the initial Western euphoria over the demise of the Soviet Union. The resurgence of the Communist Party during early 1996 stirred anxieties around the world. While now more skeptical about the tenets of Marxism, the Communists and many others will continue to rail at the loss of Russia's international stature, the disintegration of the Slavic core of the old Soviet Union, the war in

Chechnya, and above all the economic shock therapy that has cast tens of millions of Russians into poverty.

Clearly, the 1996 elections have served as a wake-up call for Westerners to recognize that Russia could easily slip into the grasp of leaders bent on reasserting the military might of the country. These firebrands, so far shackled only by financial realities and a distrustful electorate, are unimpressed by calls for joint attacks on global energy and environmental problems and the dangers of weapons proliferation.

Even less extreme opinion has become disenchanted with the American advocacy of privatization at any price and with the continued U.S. promotion of the reforms developed under Yegor Gaidar. They resent the haughty attitude of those Russians who embraced American objectives while belittling the opposition as intellectual inferiors. And the emergence of a society of haves and have-nots has dampened many an erstwhile enthusiast of the capitalist economy. Despite the persistent economic plight of Russia, they are not eager to turn westward again, even for infusions of desperately needed capital.[1]

Thus, the day is rapidly arriving when more than money will be required to launch cooperative projects—although money will continue to be important. It has become all too easy for the opponents of cooperation in the Duma and elsewhere to single out international projects that have skirted Russian law, that have lined the pockets of Russians with mafia ties while contributing little to the broader good, and that have placed Russian institutions in an inferior position with respect to their Western partners. These types of relationships imperil all cooperation.

In some ways, cooperative programs based on science and technology are among the most politically acceptable foreign activities. Science and technology projects certainly do not carry the political baggage associated with Western projects designed to influence the mass media, improve the judiciary system, or accelerate the economic reform process. They do raise concerns, however, over jeopardizing military secrets and giving away Russian technology that reflects billions of dollars of investments during Soviet times.

As to large joint projects, those that enjoy the official endorsements of government agencies—particularly the Ministry of Defense or the other power ministries—and have the signed documents to prove it should withstand political change more easily than those that are based on understanding and trust or on the enthusiasm of weaker ministries. At the other extreme, very small projects that can be characterized as people-to-people with minimal bureaucratic involvement should also have significant staying power.

The most likely future scenario will be a gradual diminution of support in Moscow among changing political leaders for cooperative projects of questionable value to Russia rather than an immediate disruption of joint endeavors. Those projects that are firmly rooted in Russia, with broad-based constituencies and official endorsements, will survive this erosion better than projects in the hands of an intellectual elite that no longer enjoys strong support within government circles.

MITIGATING THE COUNTERCURRENTS AT HOME

The path of least resistance for Washington politicians in responding to the political U-turns in Russia is curtailment of government funding for supporting various activities in the country. For starters, the large foreign aid budget is already being sharply reduced. Fortunately, in many science and technology ventures, relatively small budgets can go a long way.

Some will argue that the decline in American support will be offset by increases in the size of the Russian portfolios of the World Bank and European Bank for Reconstruction and Development. Of course, the banks have much greater financial resources at their disposal, but they do not have comparable experience nor are they charged with responsibility for promoting American interests in Russia at a time when modest investments can reap immeasurable returns.

Thus, in their zeal for budget cutting, American politicians should not forget that specialists, operating from a substantial funding base, have had a significant impact in reducing the likelihood of the spread of nuclear and missile technologies from Russia. Unfortunately, the job of containing these technologies within the country has just begun, and preventing the diffusion of the chemical and biological technologies that may be even more attractive targets for international terrorists is only now reaching the agenda for cooperation. Russian counterparts will not be able to carry the burden alone in these areas for at least several more years.

Nor should the politicians forget that Russia has been the birthplace of many scientific advances that have propelled international science during the past five decades. While Russia's research capabilities are beginning to rust, they can still be selectively polished to contribute to broad, international scientific objectives.

Finally, American leaders must recognize that the health and well-being of the United States—from the Arctic regions of Alaska to the forested areas of the Northwest to the fisheries of New England—are tightly entwined with environmental conditions in Russia. It is much easier to attack the problems of disease, insects, and pollution at their sources than after they cross the borders of the United States; in the longer term, the cleanliness of Russia's factories and the soundness of her forests will bear directly on the global climate.

As during the cold war, cooperation in science and technology can open many routes into a society straining to find its place in the world. But unlike the past, when U.S. intelligence agencies were the organizations most interested in peeking behind closed doors, today a whole array of American institutions are prepared to enter through the portals of discovery to develop projects that will bring direct benefits back to the United States. In short, science and technology bonds between the two countries can serve as an inexpensive insurance policy since joint efforts toward peace and higher standards of living in both countries will likely survive even the most stunning upsets in the daily races among Russian political leaders toward the winner's circle.

We need not rely on political tipsters when we can put our money on a sure thing.

APPENDIXES

Appendix A

U.S. Investments in Science and Technology Projects with Russia

(Funds Budgeted from January 1992 to September 1996, in millions of dollars)

U.S. Government Funds	$ Millions	Private-Sector Funds	$ Millions
Department of Defense			
Nunn-Lugar Program (chemical destruction, fissile material storage and protection, selected defense conversion activities, science centers, CRDF, Arctic activities, communications links, and others)	450	U.S. industry investment in aerospace, engineering, and other technology-intensive activities	1,500
		U.S. industry contracts and grants with Russian R&D institutions	100
Purchases of Russian technologies (SV-300 missile, Topaz space reactors, and others)	150	Various Soros funds	200
Other cooperative projects (See Appendix C)	150	Soros internal/external Internet project	100
		Other U.S. foundations	50
Department of Energy			
Protection of fissile material	160	American universities and other research institutions (their costs in addition to funds provided by U.S. government)	50
Nuclear safety	90		
Industrial partnership program	75		
Other cooperative projects (funded primarily through the national laboratories)	75		

NASA

Mir Space Station-related	400
Alpha Project	200
Other projects (See Chapter 2)	250

Freedom Support Act

Selected aspects of energy, environment, defense conversion, and health projects	275
Training and support activities	75

Other

Trade and investment: Selected expenditures of TDA, OPIC, Commerce, but does not include loans	125
Research: NSF, NIH, USDA, NIST, State, Transportation	125

Notes: Most estimates are discussed in the text and footnotes. Also, the annual and quarterly reports of the Coordinator for Assistance with the Newly Independent States of the Former Soviet Union present many additional budget details. Discussions with representatives of the concerned U.S. government agencies, U.S. companies and foundations, the U.S. Embassy in Moscow, and other observers of bilateral activities suggest that the total estimate of $4.6 billion may be too low by as much as 25 percent. However, it was not possible to document the precise amounts of relevant expenditures, particularly those by AID and by the private sector.

APPENDIX B

MISSION TO PLANET EARTH ACTIVITIES INVOLVING RUSSIA
(SUMMARY OF HIGHLIGHTS)

ATMOSPHERIC CHEMISTRY STUDIES/FLIGHT PROGRAMS

SAGE III and TOMS: Joint flights of two U.S. ozone monitoring instruments aboard separate Russian Meteor-2M spacecraft are scheduled in 1998 and 2000.

Lite Shuttle Mission: A Russian scientist is an official investigator in analyzing data from the U.S. shuttle mission of the Lidar In-space Technology Experiment, which made measurements of the earth's atmosphere and clouds in September 1994.

Correlative Measurements of Ozone: A joint implementation team studies atmospheric chemistry and physics associated with U.S. and Russian satellite-borne sensors.

LAND BIOSPHERE STUDIES

Siberian AVHRR Stations and TAIGA: NASA has loaned three high resolution picture transmission satellite data receiving stations to Russia to assist in the reception and processing of data from the spaceborne Advanced Very High Resolution Radiometer instrument aboard NOAA's polar orbiting weather satellites, with the data used to assess forest health and monitor forest fires.

FIFE-Kursk Field Experiments: Joint analysis and synthesis are continuing of data from the 1989 field campaign in Kansas (FIFE) and the 1991 field campaign in Kursk to study climatologically significant land surface parameters using satellite data.

BOREAS Field Experiment: A Russian scientist is participating in the analysis of data from the joint U.S.-Canada experiment to investigate the biological and physical processes that govern the exchange of carbon, water, trace gases, energy, and heat between boreal forest ecosystems and the atmosphere.

OCEAN STUDIES

SeaWiFS: A Russian scientist is a principal investigator in the U.S. Wide Field-of-view Sensor ocean color program to measure phytoplankton in efforts to understand the role of the oceans in the global carbon cycle.

APLE: A joint aircraft mission off the coast of Virginia was conducted in August 1996 and utilized a Russian Airborne Polarization Lidar along with NASA's Airborne Oceanographic Lidar and passive solar instruments to study global oceanic chlorophyll and chromophoric dissolved organic matter distributions.

SOLID EARTH STUDIES

Kamchatka Volcanological Studies: Russian and American scientists are jointly analyzing data obtained in the fall of 1993 from NASA and Russian aircraft that surveyed volcanoes and geothermal areas on the Kamchatka Peninsula.

Space Geodesy: This U.S.-Russian-Ukrainian effort in Very Long Baseline Interferometry geodetic experiments includes the use of a NASA-loaned Mark-3 data acquisition system in St. Petersburg and the RT-22 radiotelescope in the Crimea to study movement in the earth's crust.

Crustal Deformation in Tien Shan: This program involving specialists from the United States, Russia, Kazakstan, and Kyrgyzstan seeks to determine rates of crustal deformation and mountain building in the Tien Shan region using Global Positioning System satellites and receivers.

RADAR DATA EXCHANGE

Analyses are being conducted of data obtained during a NASA/German shuttle mission in 1994 involving the use of a synthetic aperture radar system, with Russia having provided ground truth and calibration assistance.

MIR-PRIRODA

Comparison of Atmospheric Chemistry Sensors: Using OZON-Mir 4 and Istok 1 instruments aboard Priroda, the project is defining a process whereby Russian and U.S.-based atmospheric chemistry measurements can be compared.

Calibration and Validation of Priroda Microwave Radiometers: This project will document and verify the calibration and stability of the Priroda microwave radiometers.

Validation of Priroda Rain Observations: Using data from Priroda radar, microwave, and visible/infrared radiometer data, this project will provide validation support to obtain coincident satellite and ground-based measurements of a full range of convective and stratiform rain systems in central Florida.

Global Environmental Monitoring: Using data from several Priroda sensors and from imagery and observations from the space shuttle, studies will be carried out of global change in the Aral Sea, Galveston Bay, South Florida/Bahamas, and the Panama Canal Zone.

Biosphere-Atmosphere Interchange Model of Northern Prairies: Russian Priroda data will provide valuable calibration information for the testing of the new M-BATS system over the Sioux Falls area.

Regional and Temporal Variation of Primary Productivity: This project will study the discrepancy between ship and satellite estimates of global ocean production by measuring production in shelf waters and testing regional algorithms using imagery from Priroda and NASA and NOAA satellites.

OPERATIONAL ACTIVITIES (NOAA)

NOAA and Roshydromet cooperate in the broadcast, exchange, and analysis of environmental satellite data with important implications for fields as varied as meteorology, vegetation study, atmospheric research, and analysis of sea and ice conditions.

Source: NASA, August 1996

APPENDIX C

DEPARTMENT OF DEFENSE UNITS INVOLVED IN JOINT ACTIVITIES WITH RUSSIAN INSTITUTIONS

DEPARTMENT OF DEFENSE

Armed Forces Institute of Pathology
Armed Forces Radiobiology Research Institute
Ballistic Missile Defense Organization
Defense Advanced Research Projects Agency
Defense Special Weapons Agency
Office of International Environmental Security

DEPARTMENT OF THE ARMY

Armaments Research, Development, and Engineering Center
Aviation and Troop Command
Army Medical Research Institute of Infectious Diseases
Army Research Laboratory
Army Research Office
Cold Regions Research and Engineering Laboratory
Electronics Research, Development, and Engineering Center
Missile Command
Tank and Automotive Command
Test and Evaluation Command

DEPARTMENT OF THE AIR FORCE

Air Force Office of Scientific Research
Armstrong Laboratory
Arnold Engineering Development Center
Brooks Air Force Base
European Office of Aerospace Research and Development
Kelly Air Force Base
Phillips Laboratory
Rome Laboratory
Wright Laboratory

DEPARTMENT OF THE NAVY

Naval Air Warfare Center
Naval Research Laboratory
Naval Ship Research and Development Center
Naval Surface Warfare Center
Naval Undersea Warfare Center
Navy Oceanographic Office
Office of Naval Research
Stennis Space Center

Source: This list includes those units involved in *non*-Nunn Lugar activities considered to be "cooperation in science and technology." Most of the entries were provided by officials of the Department of Defense who are familiar with activities during 1995 and 1996, with an estimated U.S. commitment of $55 million during that period. Other entries were obtained from other government officials knowledgeable about a broad range of science and technology cooperative programs. The list is believed to be about 90 percent complete for the 1992 to 1996 period.

APPENDIX D

U.S. GOVERNMENT SUPPORT OF INDUSTRIAL ACTIVITIES
(EXAMPLES OF PROGRAMS AND PROJECTS)

DEPARTMENT OF COMMERCE

- The Special American Business Internship Training Program (SABIT) offers training opportunities within American firms for Russian managers and scientists who are in positions to assist in the introduction of management practices essential for a market economy.

- The Business Information Service for the Newly Independent States (BISNET) provides information on doing business in Russia, including the frequent changes in the legal and regulatory framework, and distributes information on specific opportunities for working with Russian enterprises and applied research institutes.

- The American Business Centers in Russia provide American companies with business development and facilitation services and assist Russian firms in business training.

- Health-Industry Partnerships organize business development missions and receive trade missions to assist companies interested in medical equipment, pharmaceuticals, and health services.

- Export Control Advice is provided to Russian officials to assist them in developing an export control regime for dual-use technologies that will be consistent with international regimes and thereby reduce barriers to trade and commerce.

Source: U.S. Government Assistance and Cooperative Activities with the Newly Independent States of the Former Soviet Union, FY 1995 Annual Report, Office of the Coordinator of U.S. Assistance to the NIS, April 1996. Also, author interviews with representatives of the Department of Commerce, July 1996.

OVERSEAS PRIVATE INVESTMENT CORPORATION (OPIC)

- Conoco's "Polar Lights" oil and gas joint venture on the Barents Sea.

- The oil well restoration project in Western Siberia of Texaco International Operations.

- Pratt and Whitney's joint venture in Perm to produce commercial aircraft engines.

- Renovation and expansion undertaken by Hamilton Standard of manufacturing facilities for heating and air conditioning systems for aircraft.

- Lockheed Missiles and Space Company's joint venture with the Khrunichev and Energia firms to build a commercial satellite launch platform.

Source: Expanding America's Market, annual report, Overseas Private Investment Corporation, Washington, D.C., 1995.

TRADE AND DEVELOPMENT AGENCY (TDA)

- Conversion of former nuclear submarine shipyards to production of offshore oil platforms, one at Komsomolsk-na-Amur and one at Severodvinsk.

- Co-production of diesel engines for agricultural and other civilian uses.

- Manufacture of rechargeable batteries and photovoltaic cells.

- Production of gas turbines to be used in power generation.

- Scrapping of nuclear-powered ships at the Baltic Shipyard.

- Co-production of radars for air traffic control, and upgrading air traffic control in the Far East.

- Environmental improvements at the Magnitogorsk Metallurgical Plant.

- Modernization of the Volgograd Aluminum Smelter

Source: "U.S. Trade and Development Agency in the Newly Independent States," information sheet released by the U.S. Trade and Development Agency, January 1996.

APPENDIX E

MEMBERS OF GORE-CHERNOMYRDIN COMMISSION
(AS OF APRIL 1, 1996)

SPACE

NASA Administrator Daniel Goldin
General Director, Russian Space Agency, Yuri Koptev

BUSINESS DEVELOPMENT

Secretary of Commerce Ron Brown
Deputy Prime Minister Oleg Davydov

ENERGY POLICY

Secretary of Energy Hazel O'Leary
Minister for Atomic Energy Viktor N. Mikhailov
Minister of Fuel and Power Yuri K. Shafranik

DEFENSE CONVERSION

Secretary of Defense William Perry
First Deputy Minister of Defense Andrei Kokoshin
Chief of the Department of Defense Industries, Office of the Prime
    Minister, Valeriy A. Mikhailov

SCIENCE AND TECHNOLOGY

OSTP Director Jack Gibbons
Minister of Science Boris Saltykov

ENVIRONMENT

EPA Administrator Carol Browner
Minister of Environmental Protection and Natural Resources
    Victor Danilov-Danilyan

HEALTH

Secretary of Health Donna Shalala
Minister of Health and Medical Industry Alexander Tsaregorodtsev

AGRIBUSINESS

Secretary of Agriculture Dan Glickman
Deputy Prime Minister Aleksandr Zaveryukha

Source: "Fact Sheet, U.S.-Russian Joint Commission on Economic and Technological Cooperation (Gore-Chernomyrdin Commission)," Bureau of Public Affairs, U.S. Department of State, April 5, 1996.

APPENDIX F

AGREEMENTS REACHED BY THE
GORE-CHERNOMYRDIN COMMISSION
(JULY 1996)

SIGNED BY THE VICE PRESIDENT AND THE PRIME MINISTER:

- Memorandum of Understanding on Cooperation in Natural and Man-made Disasters, Technological Prevention and Response

- Statement of Intent on Joint Implementation of Measures to Reduce Emissions of Greenhouse Gases

- Joint Statement on Implementation of the U.S.-Russian Special Environmental Initiative

- The Schedule for the Development and Deployment of the Elements of the International Space Station

SIGNED BY COMMITTEE CHAIRS AND OTHERS:

- Memorandum of Understanding for the Support and Development of Small Business

- Joint Statement on New Cooperative Activities under the U.S.-Russia Business Development Committee

- Work plan of the Subgroup on Combating Crime of the Business Development Committee

- Protocol of the Subgroup on Financial and Banking Services of the Business Development Committee

- Joint Statement on Control, Accounting, and Physical Protection of Nuclear Materials

- Joint Statement on Nuclear Materials Protection, Control, and Accounting during Transportation

- Joint Statement on Cooperation in the Development of Clean Energy Industries

- Memorandum of Understanding on Cooperation in the Physical, Chemical, and Engineering Sciences

- Joint Statement on the *ad referendum* Agreement on the Text of a Memorandum of Understanding for the International Space Station

- Statement of Intent on Cooperation in Addressing Capital Markets Development

SIGNED IN COMMITTEE SESSION:

- Report of the Fourth Meeting of the Gore-Chernomyrdin Health Committee

- Second Joint Declaration on Children and Youth Health Promotion

- Report of Health Committee Ad Hoc Working Group on Investment in Health

- Report of the Activities of the Agribusiness Committee

- Report of the S&T Committee

- Defense Conversion Committee Report

- Recording of the May 29-30 Environment Committee Meeting

ISSUED STATEMENTS:

- Joint Statement on Human Space Flight and Science Cooperation

- Joint Statement on Aeronautics and Space Cooperation

- Statement on Civilian Research and Development Foundation Program in Biomedical and Behavioral Sciences

- Statement Announcing Formation of the U.S.-Russia Capital Markets Advisory Forum

- Joint Statement on Priority Energy Projects

- Memorandum on Discussions of the Inter-Ministerial Working Group on Oil Industry Taxation

- Joint Statement on the Protection of Intellectual Property Rights in Science and Technology Cooperation with Attachment on the Non-Binding Guidelines for Contracts and Agreements in the Field of Science and Technology

PRIVATE-SECTOR SIGNINGS:

- OPIC Finance Commitment (Chase Manhattan Bank Credit Facility)

- Lucent-COMCOR Joint Venture Agreement

- Lazare Kaplan International with Almazy Rossii-Sakha

- TDA Grant Agreement on Non-Asbestos Brake Shoes for Railway Cars

- TDA Letter of Acknowledgement of Grant Agreement on CFC Phaseout

Source: "Agreements Reached by the Gore-Chernomyrdin Commission," press release, Office of the Vice President, July 16, 1996.

APPENDIX G

MANDATE OF PRESIDENT'S COORDINATOR FOR ASSISTANCE

. . . to assure maximum coordination of efforts to promote such reforms and policies within the executive branch, I hereby designate Richard L. Morningstar as Special Adviser to the President and to the Secretary of State on Assistance to the Newly Independent States of the former Soviet Union and Coordinator of U.S. Assistance to the NIS in accordance with Section 102 of the Freedom Support Act. Mr. Morningstar will also act as Chairman of the previously established interagency NIS Assistance Coordination Group. In fulfilling these duties, Mr. Morningstar will preside over the allocation of U.S. assistance resources and direct and coordinate the interagency process on the development, funding, and implementation of all U.S. Government bilateral assistance and trade and investment programs related to the NIS.

To ensure that Mr. Morningstar will be able to carry out his responsibilities effectively, the Departments of Defense, Treasury, Justice, Commerce, Agriculture, Health and Human Services, and Energy, the Agency for International Development, United States Information Agency, National Aeronautics and Space Administration, Nuclear Regulatory Commission, Overseas Private Investment Corporation, Trade and Development Agency, and Export-Import Bank, and any other Executive departments and agencies with activities related to NIS bilateral assistance and export and investment activities are directed, to the extent permitted by law, to bring all programs and budget plans for such assistance and activities to Mr. Morningstar for review before submission to the Office of Management and Budget and before implementation. Mr. Morningstar shall be responsible for ensuring that all such plans are consistent with Administration priorities and policies. Heads of such entities shall designate an official at the level of Assistant Secretary or its equivalent to assist Mr. Morningstar in accomplishing the objectives of this mandate.

Mr. Morningstar will work with the U.S. Ambassadors to the NIS to strengthen coordination mechanisms in the field and increase the effectiveness of our assistance and export and investment programs on the ground. Assistance activities in the field will be coordinated by Ambassadors and their designates.

Mr. Morningstar will serve as a member of and consult with the Gore-Chernomyrdin Commission and the Policy Steering Group for the New Independent States to ensure that U.S. assistance and related activities are consistent with and support broader foreign policy objectives.

In carrying our these duties, Mr. Morningstar will report to me through the Assistant to the President for National Security Affairs and the Secretary of State, with policy guidance from the Policy Steering Group on the Newly Independent States.

Signed,
William J. Clinton

Source: Extract from White House Memorandum for the Heads of Executive Departments and Agencies on Charter for Special Adviser to the President, April 4, 1995.

APPENDIX H

U.S.-RUSSIAN SCIENCE AND TECHNOLOGY AGREEMENTS
(WITH SUBSIDIARY AGREEMENTS)

AGREEMENT ON SCIENCE AND TECHNOLOGY (S&T) COOPERATION (DECEMBER 16, 1993)

Memorandum of Understanding (MOU) between the Bureau of Mines and Moscow State Mining University on Cooperation in the Fields of Mining Research and Mineral Information (December 1993)

MOU Between the U.S. Forest Service and the Russian Forest Service on Cooperation in the Field of Forestry (May 1994)

NSF-Academy of Sciences MOU on Cooperation in the Field of Basic Scientific Research (June 1994)

Agreement Between Marine Mineral Service and Committee on Geology and Use of Underground Resources (June 1994)

Agreement between the USGS, Committee on Geology and Use of Underground Resources, and Russian Academy of Sciences on Cooperation in Geoscience (June 1994)

Department of Transportation-Ministry of Transportation MOU on Cooperation in Transportation S&T (June 1994)

NIH-Academy of Sciences MOU on Cooperation in the Field of Basic Biomedical Research (June 1994)

Department of Defense-Ministry of Defense MOU on S&T Cooperation in Acoustic Thermometry of Ocean Climate (December 1994)

NIST-Academy of Sciences MOU on Cooperation in the Physical, Chemical, and Engineering Sciences (July 1996)

USGS-Geodesy and Cartography Service MOU on Cooperation in the Mapping Sciences (May 1991—grandfathered into new S&T umbrella agreement)

AGREEMENT ON COOPERATION IN THE FIELDS OF PUBLIC HEALTH AND
BIOMEDICAL RESEARCH (JANUARY 1994)

AGREEMENT ON COOPERATION IN RESEARCH ON RADIATION EFFECTS
FOR THE PURPOSE OF MINIMIZING THE CONSEQUENCES OF RADIOACTIVE
CONTAMINATION ON HEALTH AND THE ENVIRONMENT (JANUARY 1994)

AGREEMENT ON COOPERATION IN THE FIELD OF PROTECTION OF THE
ENVIRONMENT AND NATURAL RESOURCES (JUNE 1994)

AGREEMENT ON S&T COOPERATION IN THE FIELD OF FUELS AND
ENERGY (JUNE 1992)

> Memorandum of Cooperation (MOC) in the Field of Fossil
> Energy between DOE and the Ministry of Fuels and Energy
> (September 1993)

AGREEMENT CONCERNING COOPERATION IN THE EXPLORATION AND USE
OF OUTER SPACE FOR PEACEFUL PURPOSES (1992)

> MOU on Cooperation in Fundamental Aeronautical Sciences
> between NASA and the State Committee for the Defense
> Branches of Industry (December 1993)

> MOU on Cooperation Relating to the Space Biomedical
> Center for Training and Research in Russia between NASA,
> the Ministry of Science, and the Russian Space Agency (June
> 1995)

AGREEMENT ON SCIENTIFIC AND TECHNICAL COOPERATION IN THE FIELD
OF PEACEFUL USES OF ATOMIC ENERGY

> MOC in the Field of Civilian Nuclear Reactor Safety

> MOC in the Fields of Environmental Restoration and Waste
> Management

> MOC on Magnetic Fusion Energy

> MOC on the Fundamental Properties of Matter

MOU ON THE PARTICIPATION OF THE **USSR** IN THE OCEAN DRILLING PROGRAM AS A REGULAR MEMBER (MAY 1991)

MOU ON S&T COOPERATION IN THE FIELDS OF STANDARDS AND METROLOGY BETWEEN **NIST** AND THE COMMITTEE FOR STANDARDIZATION AND METROLOGY (MARCH 1993)

MOU ON COOPERATION IN TELECOMMUNICATIONS (FEBRUARY 1994)

MOU ON THE GLOBAL INFORMATION INFRASTRUCTURE INITIATIVE (JULY 1994)

AGREEMENT ON COOPERATION IN OCEAN STUDIES (1990)

This partial list of bilateral arrangements includes those agreements that are considered by the Department of State to be at the level of an "international agreement" as of September 1996. There are many other agreements, memoranda, and contracts between U.S. agencies and Russian counterparts in a wide variety of fields as suggested throughout the text of this book.

Source: Department of State, September 1996.

APPENDIX I

EXEMPTION FROM RUSSIAN TAX FOR FOREIGN GRANTS

The law of the Russian Federation entitled "On Income Taxes for Individuals," which entered into force on June 21, 1996, included the following description of grants exempted from personal income tax as a subparagraph to paragraph 1 of article 3:

> ... 12) sums received by individuals as grants (gratuitous aid) for support of science and education, culture, and the arts in the Russian Federation and provided by international and foreign agencies as well as international and foreign not-for profit and charitable institutions (foundations), registered in the appropriate manner and mentioned in the lists confirmed by federal agencies of the Executive responsible for science and technological policy as well as for education, culture and the arts in the Russian Federation."

The amendment affects relations set since January 1, 1995.

Source: Civilian Research and Development Foundation, June 26, 1996, which received the information by fax from the International Science Foundation office in Moscow.

APPENDIX J

CUSTOMS EXEMPTION FOR COOPERATION IN SPACE

The following extract is from the "Agreement between the Governments of the United States of America and the Russian Federation Concerning the Procedures for the Customs Documentation and Duty-Free Entry of Goods Transported within the Framework of U.S.-Russian Cooperation in the Exploration and Use of Space for Peaceful Purposes," signed by Vice President Gore and Prime Minister Chernomyrdin and subsequently ratified by the Russian parliament:

ARTICLE 3. CUSTOMS DOCUMENTATION AND DUTY-FREE ENTRY

All goods, technologies, and software moving across the borders of the United States of America and the Russian Federation for the purposes of cooperation in space (including the Space Station program) will be entered at customs agencies, or will be exported as appropriate, in accordance with national laws and regulations, except as provided in this Article.

The Parties will provide for the import and export of goods, technologies, and software for the purpose of cooperation in space (including the Space Station program) free from the duties and taxes which the customs agencies of the Parties are otherwise legally required to impose or from which exemptions are provided by law.

In addition, the Parties will work to reduce processing fees and other similar levies which may affect imports and exports under the agreement.

ARTICLE 4. ADDITIONAL AGREEMENTS

The Parties note that certain goods, technologies, and software, necessary for implementing the "Agreement between the United States of America and the Russian Federation Concerning Cooperation in Exploration and Use of Space for Peaceful Purposes," dated June 17, 1992, and subsequent U.S.-Russian and NASA-RSA agreements concerning development of cooperation in space, may be delivered as duty free technical assistance, when for purposes of determining the possibilities of joint work in various areas of space exploration for peaceful purposes.

Source: U.S. Department of State, April 1996.

APPENDIX K

GUIDELINES ON PROTECTION OF INTELLECTUAL PROPERTY RIGHTS

These guidelines may be applied in the negotiation of contracts or agreements between United States and Russian governmental organizations, at their discretion, where such contracts or agreements are aimed at carrying out scientific or technical work for the purpose either of obtaining new scientific results, or developing prototypes of new products, or developing new technologies.

The guidelines are not binding and, when used, they shall be interpreted and applied consistent with the laws of each party.

These guidelines facilitate achievement of goals envisioned by agreements between the United States and the Russian Federation in the field of science and technology cooperation.

For the purposes of these guidelines, the term "intellectual property" shall have the meaning found in Article 2 of the Convention Establishing the World Intellectual Property Organization, done at Stockholm, July 14, 1967.

1. *Scope of Contract and Agreement Provisions on Intellectual Property:* Contracts and agreements should include provisions to cover all intellectual property whose transfer, use, dissemination or creation pursuant to the agreement or contract is reasonably foreseeable. Particular types of intellectual property of concern should be specified.

2. *Background Intellectual Property:* Before a contract or agreement is signed, parties should identify background intellectual property of relevance to the contract or agreement and provide protection for it as necessary.

3. *Protection and Allocation of Rights:* Contracts and agreements should provide for the protection and allocation of intellectual property rights resulting from the relevant contracts or agreements. In determining the allocation of rights, the parties should consider various factors, including:

   • the nature of the agreement;

- the financial and other contributions of each party, including background intellectual property;

- the intent, commitment and ability of each party to protect the resulting intellectual property; and

- the proposed participation of each party in the commercialization of intellectual property (including joint participation in commercialization, where appropriate).

In contracts and agreements, in allocating rights, the parties should take into consideration and, as necessary, indicate:

- the entities receiving rights to intellectual property derived from the contract or agreement;

- the type and extent of rights of the parties to use intellectual property in the territories of the United States and the Russian Federation and also in the territories of other countries;

- the extent of the rights of parties to use specified background intellectual property;

- the rights of one party in the event the other party fails to fulfill its obligations to obtain intellectual property protection and maintain it in force;

- the parties' right to use and obligation to protect business-confidential and proprietary information;

- the terms and procedure for transfer, exchange and publication of data generated under the contract or agreement.

4. *Protection of Business-Confidential Information:* Contracts and agreements should provide for the protection of business-confidential information specifically identified in the contract or agreement. Contracts and agreements should also include provisions specifying the conditions under which

business-confidential information may be disseminated to third parties.

5. *Inventor and Author Compensation:* Each party should provide appropriate compensation to its own inventors and authors, including, where appropriate, royalties or other income generated from its exploitation of the intellectual property which it owns and which was created by the inventor or author.

6. *Patent Application Filing Priority:* Contracts and agreements should establish patent application filing priorities in the following manner:

    • patent applications for inventions created in the United States should be filed first with the U.S. Patent and Trademark Office;

    • patent application for inventions created in Russia should be filed first with the Russian Patent Office.

    Applications should be filed in a manner consistent with 35 U.S.C. sec. 184 or art. 35 of the Patent Law of Russia, respectively.

7. *Compliance with Export Control Regimes:* Before a contract or agreement is signed, the parties should identify whether export-controlled goods, data, or services will be transferred pursuant to the contract or agreement. Parties to contracts and agreements should ensure that any transfer of goods, data, or services thereunder take place in accordance with the export control regimes of their respective countries.

8. *Languages:* Contracts and agreements should be signed in English and Russian language texts.

9. *Dispute Resolution:* Contracts and agreements should specify suitable dispute resolution mechanisms, as appropriate.

Source: "Joint Statement on the Protection of Intellectual Property Rights in Science and Technology Cooperation," press release, Office of the Vice President, July 16, 1996.

NOTES

PROLOGUE

1. For the purposes of this book, cooperation in science and technology encompasses those programs and projects that include natural and physical scientists and engineers from the two countries as pivotal participants in their design and implementation. Of course, many projects are multidisciplinary in character and involve economists, legal experts, sociologists, and others in addition to scientists and engineers; such activities are included if the scientists and engineers are central to the success of the projects.

2. Within the Washington beltway, many budget-oriented specialists concerned with the use of public funds devote great effort to distinguishing among *authorized* funds, *appropriated* funds, *rescinded* funds, *committed* funds, *obligated* funds, *notified* funds, and *expended* funds. However, for the purposes of this book, such details do not seem necessary; indeed, they would confuse even the most sophisticated readers. Therefore, the emphasis is on public funds that have been "budgeted" by government agencies from October 1991 through September 1996, with the assumption that these funds will be expended by the end of 1997.

Since there is no separate budget category for science and technology assistance or cooperation, the estimate of $2.6 billion given is based on a review of the largest blocks of funds that have been used to support assistance and cooperation involving scientists and engineers as set forth in Appendix A.

Reports that provide an overview of the foreign assistance programs of the United States are Curt Tarnoff, "The Former Soviet Union and U.S. Foreign Aid: Implementing the Assistance Program," CRS Report to Congress no. 95–170F, Congressional Research Service, January 18, 1995; Curt Tarnoff, "The Former Soviet Union and U.S. Foreign Assistance," CRS Issue Brief no. IB95077, Congressional Research Service, January 30, 1996; and *U.S. Government Assistance and Cooperative Activities with the Newly Independent States of the Former Soviet Union*, fiscal year 1995 annual report, Office of the Coordinator of U.S. Assistance to the NIS, Washington, D.C., April 1996.

3. An up-to-date and accurate estimate of private-sector expenditures in Russia has not been available, but it is clear that these expenditures have been substantial. In February 1996, according to officials of the Russian Ministry of Foreign Economics, their statistics indicated that U.S. firms had invested about

$1 billion in joint ventures and related activities in Russia since 1992, with the bulk of this involving the use of modern engineering practices—primarily in the extractive industries and in manufacturing. One U.S. estimate for the same period was $2 billion (see *U.S. Government Assistance and Cooperative Activities).*

In April 1996, specialists at the American Embassy in Moscow stated that these estimates were much too low. They estimated the U.S. investment at $2.5 billion—in the consumer, aerospace, gas, oil, and mineral sectors, with well in excess of 50 percent targeted at securing the advanced technological and engineering approaches needed to boost production. They noted that, in addition, American companies have spent a substantial amount in investigating the technological potential of the country, in buying research and services locally, and in other activities that are not reported as investments. Of course, these estimates did not include purchase or sales of equipment that was not a component of investment activities.

As indicated in Appendix A, American foundations have spent about $350 million on science and technology activities in Russia. The sixty or more U.S. universities with partnership programs in Russia have also spent considerable funds in addition to the grants they have acquired from AID and USIA, which frequently cover less than 50 percent of the actual costs of the programs. In addition, American professional societies, trade associations, and charitable organizations have spent tens of millions of dollars on activities in Russia that directly involve scientists and engineers.

4. Author interviews with Russian officials in Moscow, St. Petersburg, Nizhniy Novgorod, and Yekaterinburg, 1993–95.

5. Russian officials are unimpressed by what would appear to be large commitments of U.S. government funds to joint projects, arguing that only a very small percentage of the funds is actually expended in Russia. They contend that their own costs, in terms of the level of Russian manpower recruited and the devoting of Russian facilities to projects, far exceed the U.S. contributions, even though cost comparisons are simply not possible given the different economic situations in the two countries.

6. There are no statistics readily available on these categories of expenditures, even within individual programs. Nevertheless, the breakdown is important; these estimates are offered based on reviews of details of a number of the principal programs identified in Appendix A.

7. Ibid.

8. Ibid.

9. In November 1994, a representative of the Russian Ministry of Science and Technology Policy announced at a conference in St. Petersburg that more than one-third of *active* civilian research projects involved foreign collaborators. This fraction has undoubtedly increased during the past two years. Ministry officials informally agreed with the estimate of one-half during the spring of 1996 even though their latest data indicate that only 2 percent of the total research and development budget comes from abroad, as shown in *Russian Science and Technology at a Glance: 1995,* Center for Science Research and Statistics, Moscow,

1996, p. 40. In this regard, the amount of research under way in Russia has dropped dramatically since 1992, with much of the funds used simply to keep inactive laboratories from being abandoned. Also, these statistics indicated that even a very small foreign contribution can be important in inspiring researchers to carry out research that might otherwise not be pursued.

10. Author interviews with representatives of U.S. and European foreign assistance agencies in Moscow, 1992–94. Author interviews in Washington with participants in U.S. foreign assistance efforts, 1994–96.

11. For another perspective, see U.S. General Accounting Office, "Foreign Assistance, Assessment of Selected USAID Projects in Russia," GAO/NSAID-95-156, August 1995.

12. The following funding criteria, which presumably reflect evaluation criteria, have been advocated by the U.S. Government in *U.S. Government Assistance and Cooperative Activities*, p. 5:

- Is the recipient country ready for and open to the type of change that the assistance activity is designed to facilitate, and are there willing and appropriate interlocutors who can be full partners in the endeavor?

- Does the assistance activity have a clear objective that is consistent with our core assistance objectives, as well as with foreign policy?

- Is the assistance activity able to demonstrate results, measure progress toward its intended objective, and, ideally, produce systemic change?

- Does the activity take advantage of cost-sharing (if feasible) and/or other mechanisms to improve cost-effectiveness?

- Is U.S. assistance focused on areas where we have special expertise? Can U.S. participation help leverage funding from other donors? We should encourage a division of labor among other donors, including multilateral development banks.

- Given the transitional nature of U.S. assistance, are activities easily replicable or self-sustaining, so that the impact extends beyond the life of the NIS assistance program?

CHAPTER 1

1. For a more detailed history of science and technology cooperation between the United States and the USSR, see Glenn E. Schweitzer, *Techno-Diplomacy: U.S.-Soviet Confrontations in Science and Technology* (New York: Plenum Publishing, 1989); Glenn E. Schweitzer, "Who Wins in U.S.-Soviet Science

Ventures?" *Bulletin of the Atomic Scientists*, October 1988; and Glenn E. Schweitzer, "U.S.-Soviet Scientific Cooperation: The Interacademy Program," *Technology in Society* 14, (1992): 173–85.

2. Schweitzer, *Techno-Diplomacy*, pp. 140–41.

3. *Reorientation of the Research Capability of the Former Soviet Union*, a report to the assistant to the president for science and technology (Washington, D.C.: National Academy Press, 1992).

4. *Cooperation in Science and Technology with the Federation of Russia: Experience and Programs of Selected OECD Countries*, Organization for Economic Cooperation and Development, Paris, 1994.

CHAPTER 2

1. Overviews of the principal assistance programs are presented in Curt Tarnoff, "Freedom Support Act of 1992: A Foreign Aid Program for the Former Soviet Union," CRS Issue Brief no. IB92081, Congressional Research Service, November 3, 1992, and periodic updates of this report.

2. For a recent compilation of activities, see *U.S. Government Assistance and Cooperative Activities with the Newly Independent States of the Former Soviet Union*, Office of the Coordinator of U.S. Assistance to the NIS, fiscal year 1995 annual report, Washington, D.C., April 1996. Also of interest are the quarterly updates of such annual reports.

3. See note 2 of the Prologue and Appendix A.

4. See, for example, the "Report to the Congress of the Department of State Coordinator for Assistance to the Newly Independent States of the former Soviet Union," Office of the Coordinator of U.S. Assistance to the NIS, January 14, 1994.

5. "Cooperative Threat Reduction," brochure of the U.S. Department of Defense, April 1995 and updated July 1996.

6. Ibid.

7. "U.S. Government Assistance to and Cooperative Activities with the Newly Independent States of the Former Soviet Union, April–June 1995," Office of the Special Adviser to the President on Assistance to the Newly Independent States, released at the U.S. Department of State, September 1995.

8. Ibid.

9. Ibid.

10. Ibid.

11. Ibid.

12. McKinney H. Russell, IREX Program Letter, International Research and Exchanges Board, Washington, D.C., February 27, 1996; *Newsletter*, Office for Central Europe and Eurasia, National Research Council, Washington, D.C., 1995; material provided by the Academy for Educational Development, Washington, D.C., June 1996.

13. For a preliminary analysis of manned space activities, see John M. Logsdon and Ray A. Williamson, "U.S.-Russian Cooperation in Space: A Good Bet," *Issues in Science and Technology* 11, no. 4 (Summer 1995). Also see "International Space Station Fact Sheets," available from the U.S. Embassy, Moscow, March 1996; material updated and expanded to include all aspects of NASA bilateral activities during author interviews at NASA, Washington, D.C., July–August 1996.

14. Author correspondence with U.S. Department of Defense concerning the SV-300 purchase, September 1996; David Hoffman, "Russians Wrote Atomic History for Pentagon," *Washington Post*, October 27, 1996, p. A1.

15. Author interview at Defense Special Weapons Agency, Alexandria, Va., October 1996.

16. First annual report, International Science and Technology Center (March–December 1994), Moscow, September 1995; updated with second annual report, March 1996.

17. About 50 percent of the total were engaged in those projects supported through the International Science and Technology Center, to which the United States contributed funds. The remainder were supported by a variety of other projects funded by several U.S. agencies.

18. "Working Together to Control Nuclear Material," brochure released by the U.S. Department of Energy, January 1996.

19. These activities are summarized in the documents of the Defense Conversion Committee of the Gore-Chernomyrdin Commission, available from the office of the Vice President, July 1996.

20. "Gore-Chernomyrdin Environment Committee Program Analysis," Environmental Protection Agency, Washington, D.C., November 1995; author interview at Environmental Protection Agency, Washington, D.C., July 1996.

21. Export-Import Bank of the United States, annual report, Washington, D.C., 1995.

22. *U.S. Government Assistance and Cooperative Activities*, p. 39–40, and "Defense Enterprise Fund Commitment Summary," U.S. Department of Defense, August 31, 1995.

23. See note 3 of Prologue; author interview at Commercial Section of U.S. Embassy, Moscow, April 1996.

24. See, for example, Bretton S. F. Alexander, "1995 Year in Review: A Look at the Year in the Russian Space Program," Anser Center for International Aerospace Cooperation, Alexandria, Va., January 1996; also see "Khrunichev State Research and Production Space Center Brochure," Moscow, May 1996.

25. "Aerospace Giant Energomash Flying High with U.S. Partner," *Moscow Times*, January 16, 1996, p. 7.

26. Author interviews in Moscow with representatives of Pratt and Whitney, General Electric, and Gulfstream, April 1996.

27. "Executive Summary," advertising presentation, East-West Technology Partners Ltd., Arlington, Va., August 1995; author interview at Kiser Research, Washington, D.C., November 1995.

28. Author interview with Russian diplomats who became entrepreneurs in Northern Virginia, Washington, D.C., December 1994 and April 1996, and with a representative of the Central Aerohydrodynamics Institute, Washington, D.C., December 1995.

29. International Science Foundation, annual report, Washington, D.C., 1994.

30. Building Open Societies, Soros Foundations 1994, annual report, Open Society Institute, New York, 1995.

31. "$100 Million for University Internet Centers in Russia," press release, Open Society Institute, New York, March 26, 1996.

32. For an overview of foundation activities in Russia, see Irina Dezhina, "American Charitable Foundations: Support of Scientific Research in Russia," *Mezhdunarodnoye Nauchnoye Sotrudnichestvo* (Moscow), no. 1, 1995. Also see Howard Hughes Medical Institute, annual report, Bethesda, Maryland, 1995.

33. See, for example, the letter to the White House from the American Association for the Advancement of Science, Washington, D.C., August 6, 1992.

34. Author interview with representatives of Civilian Research and Development Foundation, Washington, D.C., August 1996.

35. Author interview with board member of Civilian Research and Development Foundation, Washington, D.C., July 1996.

36. Fact sheet released by Civilian Research and Development Foundation, Washington, D.C., August 1996.

37. "Remarks by the Vice President at the Signing Ceremony with Prime Minister Chernomyrdin," press release, Office of the Vice President, September 2, 1993. For a more detailed discussion of the commission, see "Fact Sheet, U.S.-Russian Joint Commission on Economic and Technological Cooperation (Gore-Chernomyrdin Commission)," U.S. Department of State, April 5, 1996. In elaborating on the purpose of the commission at a seminar at the Carnegie Endowment in Washington, D.C., on March 19, 1996, a representative of the Office of the Vice President explained that the original purpose of the commission was not to develop projects but simply to facilitate implementation of projects that had already been developed and agreed to by agencies in the two countries. However, it seems clear that the commission has been much more pro-active and has played a significant role in encouraging agencies to agree to projects that would not have developed in its absence. Also, the existence of the commission has applied considerable pressure on AID to pay attention to areas of science and technology that would otherwise have been neglected.

38. "Remarks by the Vice President."

39. Author interviews with senior officials from five U.S. agencies involved in the Gore-Chernomyrdin Commission activities, Washington, D.C., July–August 1996.

40. Author interviews with working-level officials in eight U.S. agencies involved in the Gore-Chernomyrdin Commission activities, Washington, D.C., June–September 1996.

CHAPTER 3

1. Author's personal observations while organizing many cooperative projects in Russia from 1992 to 1996 repeatedly underscored the difficulties in moving joint projects forward.

2. For example, the Department of Commerce claims more than fifty success stories in the field of industrial conversion involving American companies. The criterion for selecting these success stories appears to be the willingness of companies to invest funds in Russia. "Chapter 9: Selected Conversion Success Stories," *Russian Defense Business Directory*, Bureau of Export Administration, U.S. Department of Commerce, 1995.

3. Author's personal observations inside and outside malfunctioning elevators in Russia from 1993 to 1996.

4. Author communication with the Gillette Company, August 1996.

5. Author interviews during several visits to the Radio Shack store on Leninskiy Prospekt, Moscow, 1994 to 1996.

6. Paul Lawrence, "Joint Ventures in Russia: Put the Locals in Charge," *Harvard Business Review*, January–February 1993; author interview at the Commercial Section of the American Embassy, Moscow, April 1996.

7. Author interviews with specialists of the Occidental Petroleum Company in Nizhnivartovsk, Russia, June 1995; author communication with Occidental Petroleum Company, August 1996.

8. Paula M. Ross, "Monsanto's Operations in the Former Soviet Union: A Case Study," in Deborah Anne Palmieri, ed., *Russia and the NIS in the World Economy: East-West Investment, Financing and Trade* (New York: Praeger, 1994); author communication with Monsanto Company, August 1996, which corrected misinformation in the original source.

9. Author interview at Boeing Research Center in Moscow, June 1994; Andrei Baev et al., "American Ventures in Russia," report of a workshop, Center for International Security and Arms Control, Stanford University, 1995, pp. 4–5; author communication with the Boeing Company, August 1996.

10. Author interviews with representatives of the Digital Equipment Corporation in Moscow, July to September 1994.

11. "Feasibility Study of Technologies for Accelerator-based Conversion of Military-Plutonium and Long-Lived Radioactive Waste," annual report, Institute of Theoretical and Experimental Physics, Moscow, November 1995; author interview with Russian project manager, Washington, D.C., February 1996.

12. Author interviews at Institute for Earthquake Prediction, Moscow, and Institute of Mechanics and Mathematics, Yekaterinburg, August 1994; author interview with a senior scientist of the project, Moscow, November 1995.

13. Author interviews at Obninsk Institute of Physics and Power Engineering, Obninsk, November 1995.

14. Baev et al., "American Ventures in Russia," pp. 9–11; author communication with Sun Microsystems, August 1996.

15. "Russian-American Electric Propulsion Systems," briefing material for presentations in Washington, D.C., October 1995, by Loral Space Communications; author communications with Loral Space Communications, August 1996.

16. Annual report, International Science Foundation (1994), Washington, D.C., June 1995; author communication with a former International Science Foundation staff member, July 1996.

17. I. A. Lerch, B. Bronnar, and J. Kirin, "The Role of the American Physical Society in Responding to the Crisis in Basic Science," paper presented at Symposium on Science, Technology, and International Security at the National Academy of Sciences, sponsored by the White House Office of Science and Technology Policy, Washington, D.C., April 1995; author communication with American Physical Society, August 1996.

18. "Supplementary Grants to Provide Infrastructural Support for Counterparts in the Former Soviet Union," fact sheet, National Science Foundation, April 8, 1992; NSF program announcement no. 96–14, National Science Foundation, Washington, D.C., January 22, 1996; author communication with National Science Foundation, August 1996.

19. Elizabeth Campos Rajs, "Putting Crystals on Fast Track," Lawrence Livermore National Laboratory, February 18, 1994, p. 1; author communication with Lawrence Livermore National Laboratory, August 1996.

20. Author interviews with U.S. Agency for International Development specialists in Moscow, November 1995; author interview with a former board member of International Science Foundation, Washington, D.C., July 1996.

21. Author interviews with a specialist from the National Marine Fisheries Service, U.S. Department of Commerce, February and August 1996.

22. "Vital and Health Statistics: Russian Federation and United States, Selected Years, 1980–93," National Center for Health Statistics, U.S. Department of Health and Human Services, June 1995; author communication with Department of Health and Human Services, August 1996.

23. "USGS Cooperative Energy Resource Programs in the Former Soviet Union, Russia: Petroleum Resource Assessment and Exploration," U.S. Geological Survey, February 1996; author communication with U.S. Geological Survey, August 1996.

24. Author interview with a NASA representative in Moscow, March 1996; author interview at NASA, Washington, D.C., August 1996.

25. Author interview with a U.S. Environmental Protection Agency official, February 1996; communication with Environmental Protection Agency, August 1996.

26. Author interview with an official of the Fish and Wildlife Service, U.S. Department of the Interior, and associated memorandum, March 1996; author communication with Fish and Wildlife Service, U.S. Department of the Interior, August 1996.

27. "Acoustic Thermometry of Ocean Climate," press release, Office of the Vice President, December 16, 1994; author interview at U.S. Department of State, March 1996.

28. Author interviews with representatives of the Russian Ministry of Defense and U.S. Department of Defense, January 1996.

29. "U.S.-Russian Special Environmental Initiative," press release, Office of the Vice President, January 30, 1996.

30. Material provided to author by McDermott, Inc., March 15, 1996.

31. Documentation provided by Cooperative Threat Reduction Program, U.S. Department of Defense, August 1996.

32. Author interview with an American expert reviewing Russian proposed technical approach, Moscow, May 1996.

33. Reports available at the National Research Council, Washington, D.C., July 1996.

34. Material provided to author by Academy for Educational Development, Washington, D.C., February 1996.

35. G. Kochetkov, "Russian Conversion in Light of World Experience in Management," *Konsultant Direktora* (Moscow), no. 7 (October 1995), pp. 3–9. Author interview at Institute for the USA and Canada, Moscow, April 1996.

36. "Russian Energy and Environmental Commodity Import Program," U.S. Agency for International Development, Moscow, November 1995; author interview at U.S. Agency for International Development, Moscow, April 1996.

CHAPTER 4

1. Comments by an influential Russian consultant to Duma members directly involved in relations with the United Sates, Washington, D.C., February 1996. While his estimate of the amount of money entering Russia under the program may have been correct at the time, since then the flow of Nunn-Lugar funds has increased significantly.

2. Howard Witt, "Russians Wary of U.S. Promises; West Failed to Deliver Billions in Aid," *Chicago Tribune*, January 12, 1994, p. 1.

3. See, for example, Marc Champion and Steve Liesman, "$24 Billion and Where Has It Gone?" *Moscow Times*, April 15, 1993, p. 1.

4. See Aleksandr Shokin's foreword, in *Structural Reform in the Russian Federation: Progress, Prospects, and Priorities for External Support*, The World Bank and the Government of the Russian Federation, Washington, D.C., April 20, 1993.

5. Leonid Abalkin, "Evaluation of USA Technical Aid in the Course of Democratic and Economic Transformations in Russia," paper presented at a seminar at George Washington University, February 28, 1996. Unfortunately, AID officials did not accept invitations to attend the seminar and comment on the allegations. However, similar comments were made by officials of three Russian ministries during author interviews in Moscow in April 1996.

6. "International Cooperation of Minatom of Russia," *Atom Press* 33, no. 179 (September 1995), p. 3.

7. Comments made by a director of a Russian nuclear weapons research institute at Macy's, Pentagon City, Virginia, January 12, 1996.

8. Glenn E. Schweitzer, *Moscow DMZ: The Story of the International Effort to Convert Russian Weapons Science to Peaceful Purposes* (Armonk, N.Y.: M. E. Sharpe, 1996).

9. Comments by the director, Institute of Biology of the North, Magadan, at a seminar at the National Research Council, Washington, D.C., February 1996.

10. "Gore-Chernomyrdin Sign Almost Thirty Documents and Promise a Jump in New Investments in Russia," *Finansoviye Izvestiya* (Moscow), July 18, 1996, p. 1.

CHAPTER 5

1. Extracted from trip reports of exchange scientists, National Research Council, Washington D.C., January 1996.

2. From 1994 to 1996, the author attended five conferences in the United States that considered U.S. foreign assistance activities in Russia. Three perennial themes raised by American scientists in attendance were (a) the difficulty of communicating with U.S. AID, (b) the lack of interest of AID in considering any ideas from outside the agency, and (c) excessive AID expenditures for some science and technology projects with little payoff. In addition, during that time many individual comments of American scientists along the same lines were repeated to the author.

3. Author discussions with more than two hundred American scientists from 1992 to 1996.

4. Paul Lawrence and Charalambos Vlachoutsicos, "Joint Ventures in Russia: Put the Locals in Charge," *Harvard Business Review*, January–February 1993, pp. 44–54.

5. *Cooperation in Science and Technology with the Federation of Russia; Experience and Programs of Selected OECD Countries*, Organization for Economic Cooperation and Development, Paris, 1994.

6. David Bernstein and Elaine Naugle, "U.S.-Russian High Technology Ventures: Lessons Learned," *Conversion*, a publication of the Center for International Security and Arms Control, Stanford University, no. 6 (1996).

7. *Cooperation in Science and Technology*. Also see "Practical Responses for Overcoming Obstacles to Cooperation," Committee for Scientific and Technological Policy, Organization for Economic Cooperation and Development, Paris, 1995.

8. Extracted from trip reports of exchange scientists, National Research Council, Washington, D.C., January 1996.

9. Author interviews with Russian officials in Moscow, St. Petersburg, Nizhniy Novgorod, and Yekaterinburg, 1993–95.

10. NASA programs reflect many examples of this approach. See Chapters 2 and 3.

11. See Chapter 3 for the experience of the Academy for Educational Development.

12. The concept of pay by the day was pioneered by the International Science and Technology Center (ISTC). While initially encountering stiff resistance from Russian scientists, who thought they were going to lose their vacation privileges and health benefits, the concept was gradually accepted after the institutes were able to make arrangements for health coverage and as the scientists realized that their paychecks were sufficiently high to cover any vacation periods.

13. The experience of the ISTC is relevant. Of the more than two hundred proposals written by American specialists for ISTC support of cooperative ventures with Russian colleagues submitted to the Department of State in 1992–1993, only three eventually resulted in officially sponsored projects, and these three were based on proposals that were substantially reshaped and then resubmitted by Russian institutions. Meanwhile, more than fifty proposals developed by Russian institutions during the same period received financial support.

14. Glenn E. Schweitzer, *Moscow DMZ: The Story of the International Effort to Convert Russian Weapons Science to Peaceful Purposes* (Armonk, N.Y.: M. E. Sharpe, 1996), Chapter 8. This book contains a number of discussions of the issue and presents the limited data that were available.

15. Author interviews with officials and scientists from dozens of Russian research institutes, 1993–1996. Representatives of American institutions providing the funds are reluctant to admit that such a large percentage of the money does not reach individual Russian scientists, but seldom can they produce documentation that shows otherwise.

16. An untitled memorandum prepared by the Commercial Section of the American Embassy in Moscow, July 1996, provides similar advice.

17. A particularly thoughtful list of lessons learned in providing foreign support for basic research programs in Russia is included in Lev Kisselev, "Areas of Current Strength in Biomedical Research in Russia," paper presented at a meeting on biomedical research in the former Soviet Union organized by the Wellcome Trust, London, October 23, 1996.

18. Author communication with the Center for Defense Information, Washington, D.C., August 1996.

19. Author interview at NASA, Washington, D.C., August 1996.

CHAPTER 6

1. For an insightful discussion of the future of foreign assistance, see Curt Tarnoff, "Russia and U.S. Foreign Assistance: Current Issues," CRS Report for Congress no. 96–261F, Congressional Research Service, March 20, 1996.

2. U.S. Department of Energy officials have expressed amazement at their success in opening new channels of communication with Russian scientists from even the most sensitive Russian facilities. NASA officials are similarly pleased

with their broad-ranging interactions with many Russian counterparts. These observations were made during author interviews in Washington and Moscow in January and April 1996.

3. For an analysis of the future of the Nunn-Lugar program, see Amy F. Wolf, "Nunn-Lugar Cooperative Threat Reduction Programs: Issues for Congress," CRS Report for Congress, no. 96–804F, Congressional Research Service, September 30, 1996.

4. Tarnoff, "Russia and U.S. Foreign Assistance."

5. One proposal that suggested a new, regionally focused agency for administering U.S. economic assistance funds for the former Soviet Union was set forth in R. E. Butler and Alexey Alexeyev, "Charting a New Course for U.S.-Russia Cooperation," report of the Utah-Russia Institute, Provo, Utah, published in *Business World of Russia Weekly* (Moscow), March 20–26, 1995, p. 2.

6. See Chapter 2.

7. Author interview with an official of the Department of State, August 1996. The three foundations deal with research in basic science (including medicine), industry, and agriculture. U.S. contributions to the three foundations date back to the early 1970s and have been primarily in the form of allowing Israel not to make scheduled and rescheduled repayments on U.S. loans. The foundations then receive payments based on the interest that is earned on the funds retained by Israel.

8. At the Gore-Chernomyrdin meeting in July 1996, the Committee for Science and Technology agreed to consider ways to enhance cooperation in commercialization of technologies, especially the mutually beneficial commercialization in the United States of technologies wholly or partially developed in Russia.

9. Author interview with officials of the Department of Energy, February 1996. The cost of sending a senior scientist from one of the national laboratories to Russia was about $1,400 per day (to cover salary, benefits, and laboratory overhead) plus direct expenses. The time involved included not only the days abroad but also days for preparatory work and for completing trip reports.

EPILOGUE

1. These views are similar to those set forth in Aleksandr Tsipko, "In Russia, a New Kind of Moral Majority," *Washington Post*, December 24, 1995, p. C1.

Index

ABOUT THE AUTHOR

Glenn Schweitzer's interest in Russian-American cooperation spans more than three decades. He was the first scientific attaché at the American Embassy in Moscow in the 1960s, and he then returned to Russia in 1992 to lead the combined efforts of the United States, the European Union, Japan, and Russia to establish the International Science and Technology Center in Moscow. After serving as the first executive director of the center, he returned in 1994 to his current position as director of the Office for Central Europe and Eurasia at the National Academy of Sciences/National Research Council. His previous books include *Techno-diplomacy: U.S.-Soviet Confrontations in Science and Technology* (Plenum, 1989) and *Moscow DMZ: The Story of the International Effort to Convert Russian Weapons Science to Peaceful Purposes* (M.E. Sharpe, 1996).